My Chilean Wine Odyssey

A Week Touring
the Wine Country of Chile

By

John R. Knuth

© 2003 by John R. Knuth. All rights reserved.

No part of this book may be reproduced, stored in a retrieval system, or transmitted by any means, electronic, mechanical, photocopying, recording, or otherwise, without written permission from the author.

ISBN: 1-4107-5425-1 (e-book)
ISBN: 1-4107-5424-3 (Paperback)

Library of Congress Control Number: 2003094303

This book is printed on acid free paper.

Printed in the United States of America
Bloomington, IN

1stBooks - rev. 06/21/03

Dedication

These pages are dedicated

to my father,

Rodney Knuth

He spent his whole life traveling

via National Geographic...

and never left home.

Also...

To my wife Carmen who

sacrificed sharing the

experiences of this trip to

be the loving and caring

mother she always will be.

Contents

Chapter 1 1
How did I Get Here?

Chapter 2 8
Getting to Chile

Chapter 3 16
Welcome to Santiago

Chapter 4 22
Lunch and Beyond

Chapter 5 29
Wine 101

Chapter 6 44
The Vineyards and Pablo

Chapter 7 53
Lunch at Hacienda Los Lingues

Chapter 8 58
Dinner with the Board

Chapter 9 63
Casablanca Valley andBeyond

Chapter 10 73
Valparaiso and Vina del Mar

Chapter 11 82
Traveling North to Zapallar

Chapter 12 88
Dinner in Vina del Mar

Chapter 13 93
Goodbye to the Pacific

Chapter 14 106
The Ride Home

Chapter 15 109
Putting it all into Perspective

Preface

I grew up in an Italian-American household. My mother was as Italian as they came and, as such, wine was never far from any family gathering. I began adding wine to my diet on a cruise I took with my wife back in the late 80's. Sutter Home White Zinfandel can be credited with starting my love affair with wine.

As I point out in my story, Morande was kind enough to pick up all the expenses associated with the ground portion of my trip. I mention this to ensure some fairness in all my "reporting." I believe my feeling towards these people, both as individuals and as a company, would not change regardless who paid what portion of the expenses.

I want to thank all those involved who graciously allowed me to use their names throughout the story. It was those individuals who added the color and texture to the trip, making it as enjoyable as it was.

If you get an opportunity to visit Chile, don't pass it up. As a matter of fact, make it a destination. You won't regret it.

So sit back and enjoy "My Chilean Wine Odyssey." Cheers.

Chapter 1

Saturday March 8, 2003

"How Did I Get Here?"

Today I start an adventure that actually began five weeks ago. Each year I host a wine dinner to benefit our local school district. This year's theme was based on the wines of Chile. In the past several years the Chilean wine industry has boomed. Many wines, some of them representing remarkable values, have been hitting the market at a expeditious pace. It was time to recognize this trend. As I considered possible wine distributors to help with the event, my thoughts turned to one of my more endearing wine vendors, Robert Morgen of Wein-Bauer. Bob has become a good friend and is most certainly a very knowledgeable individual when it comes to wine,

John R. Knuth

particularly German and Austrian wines. As a former Austrian citizen, his knowledge of the language and regions make him an excellent source of wine information. He has taught me a lot about wine, and about life, for that matter.

As weeks marched on, it was time to pick a theme for the wine dinner. Chilean wines seemed an easy choice. Menu items to match the wines would prove a challenge as I knew so little about the country, its people and its cuisine. One of the most fun aspects of the wine dinner is the pairing of wines with food items. Unlike so many other countries we read about, Chile was unusual in that my knowledge was limited to the Pinochet years of dictatorship, making Chile not a very popular place. My only other knowledge of the country came from a National Geographic Traveler magazine which laid around my house for many months. In that particular issue was a story of a woman's journey through the southern part of Chile. It seemed like an interesting place to visit. I had read the issue cover to cover several times. The Chile discussed in National Geographic was a beautiful, rugged country with much diversity in its countryside, wonderful people and great food.

My Chilean Wine Odyssey
A Week Touring the Wine Country of Chile

So, Chile was my choice and Bob Morgen was my distributor. Now I needed Bob to get a vintner and I needed to find out something about Chilean cuisine. My first try was looking for a Chilean restaurant in Chicago. No luck. Next, I went on-line looking up recipes at Food Network. Again, not much luck. Well, at about that time Bob called back saying he found someone for our dinner. My guidelines for a host are pretty simple. He must be passionate about his product., know enough about wine to be believable, and have a thick accent! Jaime Merino, pronounced "Hi Me", came from a Chilean winery known as Morande. Morande's founder was a wine maker named Pablo Morande. He became well known for the work he did at the famous Concha y Toro winery. His wines promised to be stellar examples of all Chile could offer.

I first spoke with Jaime back in October of 2002. My first recollection of my conversation with him was that the accent would work! He seemed to know his wine well and making things even better, he was a personable guy. The winery for our sixth annual dinner and wine tasting was now chosen. Over the next several weeks I got to know Jaime a little better as we began planning our menu for the dinner. Jaime seemed quite knowledgeable about his wines and the process of making a wine dinner work. He informed me that much of the cuisine of Chile is relatively bland. Beef, cheese, seafood, pork, you can just about name anything and it seems as though it appears somewhere on the menu in Chile. His country has been populated by Europeans, especially the Germans, Irish and Italians. The foods are remarkably similar to what we enjoy in the states.

Our wine dinner was scheduled for early February 2003. During the next several months I spoke often with Jaime as we worked out details of the dinner. But, my first tasting of the wines from Morande, were less than satisfying. I wasn't sure that the label would be up to the higher quality we created last year when we featured a small winery from California. I hate to take someone backwards on the long road towards the "next level" when it comes to wine. Jaime and Bob both were quite insistent that the product was indeed up to the challenge and provided me with additional samples of newer releases until I found products in the Morande line which seemed to work.

February 1 finally rolled around. The wine dinner is an event I take very personally. It represents a love of wine, some of my best friends, lots of work and a good cause, our local school, all rolled into one high pressure evening for me. I arrived at our event several hours early to begin checking on details and help open wine. We would serve almost 250 bottles of wine during the evening and opening them becomes quite a chore. Jaime arrived shortly after I did and I finally got to meet the guy. My first impression was that he was well groomed and well mannered. He proceeded to run a very nice dinner, everything I hoped it would be. He was eloquent and professional. I think he was also impressed with us as he was quite complimentary of the evening. As the evening went on, we checked in with each other from time to time and worked well together. In a wine tasting event, especially with 200 people in attendance, time and crowd volume level increase hand in hand. By 10:00 pm, things were loud and it was difficult to grab the crowd's attention between courses. Jaime stuck with it and did a great job. As the event came to a close, I approached Jaime to congratulate him on the great job he had done. During our conversation it dawned on me to seize upon a possible opportunity…"if you ever need someone to ride shotgun with you on a trip to Chile, let me know," I boldly said. Not quite sure if it was the alcohol or my desire to travel, but out came the words. I assured Jaime I would be more than happy to pick up all of my expenses. It wasn't more than several seconds before Jaime looked at me and said "How about March 8?" I must have had a perplexed look upon my face as Jaime quickly added that he could see something wasn't quite right and that I probably needed to check with my wife Carmen, who was standing ten or so feet away. He quickly added that she should come too!

John R. Knuth

We would be responsible for our air fare. Once on the ground in Chile, all expenses would be covered by Morande. Wow! A once in a life-time opportunity, and to make things even more fun, there would be no long months of waiting. This trip was only five weeks away!

As it turns out, we had planned our first big family vacation in five years and we would be getting back home late Monday night just four days before this trip was scheduled to leave. Coming home late and just having started a new job was too much for her. She teetered for several days, but I knew she would opt out. Leaving our kids was never easy, but this had too many other things to work out. Several days later, despite all my pressures to the contrary, Carmen officially bowed out. I was saddened, but knew I would still go. Brothers, friends and fellow wine lovers were all offered the opportunity for the "trip of a lifetime." Funny thing about a trip of a lifetime…seems as everyone says they would go in an instant, yet no one seemed able or willing to commit. In the end, I would take the trip with my brother and business partner, Dave So here we are. Cruising along at 35,000 feet at 4:30 in the morning. I have promised myself I would do my best to document my experiences, for Carmen, who couldn't be here, and for myself. I am told by my host, Jaime, that I will indeed have some wonderful experiences. He assured me that I would learn more about Chile and about

My Chilean Wine Odyssey
A Week Touring the Wine Country of Chile

my passion for wine in the next few days than I can imagine at this time. Santiago will be mine for the taking in only three more hours. I can't wait.

Chapter 2

Saturday March 8, 2003

Getting to Chile

Saturday, March 8, 2003. Where have the five weeks gone? The family trip to Disney World kept me busy and since our arrival back home Monday evening at 2:00 am, the week has been a blur. Getting caught up from one trip and turning around to leave on a another trip only days away, what was I thinking? I see why Carmen didn't want to go! Anyway, the weather in Chicago was typical early March. Snow and cold prevailing. The weather in Santiago was 87 degrees yesterday. I think I will muster up the energy to get going. I might be complaining a little here, but I am not nuts!

My Chilean Wine Odyssey
A Week Touring the Wine Country of Chile

Dave and I both went to work on Saturday. Dave was already at work when I got there and we proceeded to work on what had to get done. It was hard to concentrate. I was very excited as I dragged through the final checklist. We don't usually both take off work at the same time and when we do, it requires additional planning. The entire week was filled with emergency checklists, who's doing what and when. After two hours, I was done and wanted to catch my son's basketball game. I left Dave behind to finish up chores. Our departure time was slated for 11:30 am to make a 3:05 trip out of O'Hare. For anyone who has ever traveled out of O'Hare you know that the only variable at that airport is everything. You can make it from our home in as little as 45 minutes, and then again, the trip can take hours. Traffic can be as bad as you could possibly imagine, but our lead time should give us ample time for any traffic problems as well as arriving early enough to cover any delays caused by tightened security.

A quick ride through the city of Chicago went without a hitch. Traffic was light and our only potential sidetrack was looking for back-up battery packs for our laptop computers. We knew of a large computer store located only a few blocks off our trail. We tried several phone calls to stores we knew were in the area but no luck. As we arrived at O'Hare airport we entered the remote parking area. Ten or so minutes looking for a parking spot made both Dave and me feel glad we didn't take the detour for batteries. Finally, a parking spot. In section E7…far away from the tram building, but it was the best we could do. We unloaded our gear and began the long walk to the transfer train building. It was cold and damp. Making matters worse, a heavy rain began as we approached the building. Dave had found a luggage cart in the parking lot and was working his way to the building at a pretty good clip. I was trailing behind slightly pulling my bag with my carry-on bag clipped on. I didn't realize but my new bag was dragging its shoulder strap. The strap survived, showing only a little dirt as my first souvenir. The tram ride was fun. A chance to be a passenger and let someone else, in this case a computer, drive the train. Security was tight but we didn't have any problems as we worked our way through the various bag checks and x-ray machines. We checked our main suitcase directly through to Santiago. Hopefully, we would see it there, but we were first heading to Atlanta to catch up with the rest of our group. Flight 1455 was scheduled to depart O'Hare, Gate L9 at 3:05.

Gate L9 brought back a bad memory for me. It was the very gate where five years earlier I had been pick pocketed for $400 on our last family trip to Disney World. I immediately recognized the very spot where I remembered the event happened.

My Chilean Wine Odyssey
A Week Touring the Wine Country of Chile

It's five years later and I had learned my lesson. I was now wearing a money belt. Although it is warm and uncomfortable at times, I know my money is safe. We sat in the terminal playing with our electronic toys. A McDonald's down the hall filled the fare for a quick bite to eat. Our plane finally arrived a few minutes late due to the bad weather. We boarded a 757 and realized that this was going to be a tight ride. Good thing it was only supposed to be a two hour flight. Row 34, seats E and F. I think I may have claustrophobia nightmares about that flight. I tried the laptop in flight but gave up. No room to do anything. I tried to get comfortable as best as I could. Atlanta is an hour ahead of Chicago, so for the first time in the trip, I set my watch ahead a full hour. The flight was full and we left almost a half hour late, but strong upper level winds and a pilot who did a serious power-on descent made up some time and we landed in Atlanta's, Hartsfield airport about 20 minutes behind schedule.

Welcome to Atlanta. The airport seemed very full of passengers heading off all over the place. A true hub airport. We needed to find our way over to the International Terminal, Terminal E. Our plan was to go to the International Terminal Crown room and meet up with our group. A tram ride and lots of walking finally brought us to the International terminal and we soon found the Crown room. I had always wanted to go into one of these rooms, and now I knew why. Quite nice actually, a free bar, clean marble bathrooms, you get the idea.

We informed the somewhat terse woman at the front counter that we were here to meet with Jaime Merino. She pointed to a small conference room. Jaime was already inside and as always, very polite as he greeted both Dave and me. One by one members of our group began to arrive. Jaime informed us that there would be a total of nine of us making the journey to Chile.

The first person we met was Don. Don owned a wine distributorship in New Mexico. A thin gentleman in his early 50's, I'd guess. He had the southwestern thing going with a bit of silver in his belt. It turns out his belt had some history. It was made by the same guys who used to make belts for Roy Rogers and other western TV stars. It was worth a lot of money, and Don was glad no one seemed to know that. Don reminded me a bit of Sonny Triebold, my mother's friend of many years. Next to arrive was Tom. Tom was from the opposite end of the country, the northeast. Connecticut to be exact. Another wine broker. I am guessing Tom was in his 50's. Next to show up were Mike and Jim, both from Denver. Mike, the senior of the two was probably in his late 50's while Jim looked 40'ish. Mike, an Italian distributor, seemed quite likeable, a little more verbose and louder than the first two we'd met. Jim, seemed like a nice guy. Next come the two men from Atlanta, Bruce and Dave. They were the youngest of the crowd. We all introduced ourselves and exchanged business cards. A quick conversation broke out about our different angles on the business, liquor laws, new wines, etc. This was really beginning to look like a business trip. An icy cold Fosters from the free bar helped loosen me up after the tight confines of our earlier flight. As we sat around the table, a bottle of cabernet sauvignon came out of a briefcase, courtesy of the boys from Atlanta. A stack of glasses soon followed and we toasted Jaime on our upcoming adventure. The conversation slowed down and everyone seemed to go their separate ways, checking in at the bar a last time, walking the airport or hitting the bathroom. We needed to leave our room by 9:00 to check in for our international flight. Dave and I had been looking at noise-canceling headsets before we left, but never made a purchase. Dave headed out for an airport walk and came back with news of some headsets down the hall. We took off for a last minute shopping spree. The noise factor on the short ride down seemed like it could be a factor for our late night trip so we blew our first $200 on two sets of headphones. What the heck.

John R. Knuth

We were off for the terminal. The flight was booked solid, A Boeing 767-300. Our seat assignments were row 36 F and G. The coach configuration was 2, 3, 2 and we had the right two seats towards the back of the plane. Jaime told us as we arrived in Santiago in the morning that the Andes would be on the left side of the plane and the Pacific on the right. Looks like we got the ocean view. Once again we were treated to tight quarters. It was going to be a 9 ½ hour flight. The time difference was one hour ahead so my watch got pushed ahead one more time. We left Atlanta about ½ hour behind schedule due to a broken seat belt, but were notified by the captain that strong tail winds would still get us into Santiago on or ahead of schedule.

While standing in the boarding line we talked to a young college girl who had just been upgraded free of charge to first class. What a perk. The rest of us "lessers" climbed our way to the back of the plane. Full of passengers and fuel, down the runway we headed. Our flight would take us down Florida, over Cuba (where I was amazed at how dark the island was compared to the US), the Panama Canal, Peru, the Pacific and down Chile. We were scheduled to land in Santiago at 8:30 am local time. The flight down had been uncomfortable. A little turbulence and not much room to move around. We were treated to a choice of a steak or chicken dinner. I was hungry and while I am not sure the food was that great from a culinary point, it hit the spot. A piece of cheese, Rubschlager bread, a small piece of steak and mashed potatoes, small salad and strawberry shortcake for dessert. Worked for me. Breakfast would be served in a little while.

At 6:30 am we only had a couple of hours to go. I walked around the plane awhile to stretch my legs as the sky began to brighten. Within another half an hour the sky was bright blue. A thick layer of clouds was underneath us, when all of a sudden the clouds broke and we could see the shores of Chile! The landscape seemed very rugged with few roads. Valleys with small single lane roads began to appear. We were served a light breakfast consisting of a croissant, jelly and orange juice. It all tasted good, especially the coffee. I began to get restless as I knew we were getting close. Good news and bad I suppose…good in that we were almost there, bad in that I knew I had to do it again to get home. Landing was smooth and the sun shone brightly on our man made beast. Quite an amazing machine to take 200+ people 5000 miles, non-stop. One hundred years ago, the trip would have taken months, and many could have possibly died along the way. Too bad it was so cramped.

Chapter 3

Saturday/Sunday March 8 and 9

Welcome to Santiago

A short taxi to the gate and after a short delay (another plane was still in our spot) we were allowed to deplane. Santiago airport seemed small and had a unique Latin American feel to it…not in a bad way, but it was quite different from the scenes we had left in O'Hare and Atlanta. The temperature was a seasonal 63 degrees, with a high expected to reach 85. The terminal was neat and clean inside. Bustling Chileans and visitors from abroad hurried from one place to another, quite similar to O'Hare and Atlanta. Chilean natives appeared to have a slightly darker complexion but seemed quite European in their hustle and bustle, clothing, and the like. We

My Chilean Wine Odyssey
A Week Touring the Wine Country of Chile

worked our way to the first staging area for customs. US citizens must pay $100 cash entry fee for a one time visa. Some in line seemed a little surprised and headed for cash machines. Cash, travelers checks or personal checks accepted. The younger clerk quite happily took my $100 bill, smiled, stamped and stapled a receipt into my passport and I went to catch up with rest of our group. Next line was through customs where nothing out of the ordinary happened. My customs agent appeared absolutely indifferent to my presence, not stopping to say "Hello" or "Get the heck out of my country." Just a stamp, stamp, flip, flip and I was out. Meeting up with the group, it was onto luggage claim. Again a scene similar to airports across the world. Someone was complaining in Spanish about a lost bag, while others hoped that their bag would magically appear from around the mysterious turnstile. Mine did. So I was off to go through the final step, the Department of Agriculture check for plants and animals. Quite a long line that moved quickly. Again, no smirks, nor smiles for that matter as it was life in a busy airport. When our group neared the staging area, Jaime did his thing and we were allowed to pass. We once again waited for everyone in the main terminal area.

Children running, people hugging relatives, we'd all seen it a hundred times, but new to this crowd were the taxi and bus hawkers. They did their best to grab your bags and head you to their waiting taxi. Several times I had to politely say "No thank you" as someone grabbed for my bags and said "taxi." Jaime had arranged for a large tour bus to take us into Santiago, about a 30 minute ride. Once again, numerous "helpers" tried to grab my bag to my continual insistence that I took my own. A short walk outside where the air had now warmed into the 70's and our bus was waiting. The familiar cries of "five dollars, five dollars" rang from all our "assistants". I politely refused to pay one man and he reminded me of the work he did hauling my bag to the bus. I reminded him I carried my own, loaded my large suitcase into the baggage area of the bus and headed on-board with my carry-on bag.

A second seat view and we were heading for downtown Santiago on a particularly nice bus. Our driver had a cooler in the front seat. My curiosity was answered before I could ask as Jaime offered everyone a water, plain or with fizzies. I took mine plain and began looking out the window. The land reminded me of photos I've seen of Arizona, with mountains rising up in the background and what appeared to be a drier climate. The road out of the airport quickly went from a typical airport area to East L.A. Taggers seem to have control over the east side of the city as we went through some pretty tough looking neighborhoods. Not that they looked especially dangerous or mean, yet I wouldn't want to stray there late in the evening on my own. Jaime would chime out an occasional landmark as we made our way into the city. The palace, Civic Center, University of Chile (the oldest university in South America) and the train station, to name a few. Then we came upon a very attractive plaza. Jaime informed us that this spot was the informal dividing line between the "haves" and "have nots." You could instantly see that this made sense. We had entered a very modern, clean city. No graffiti here, only large office buildings and landscaped areas. We continued on into a quiet residential area where our hotel was located. A very professional staff greeted us as we pulled up. I asked Jaime about tipping and he said "not here," so I dutifully obeyed. We were introduced to several members of the Morande staff as well as the hotel staff. Jaime collected passports to photocopy for the hotel while we were lead into a conference room and given individual room assignments. Jaime gave us three hours to "freshen up" any way we liked. We were then to meet in the same conference room for a lunch and a city tour. We signed our names onto a hotel form and were given our room keys, which were the credit card-type swipe cards. My room was 204, right by the stairs. I went to grab my bag and was told it would be brought up momentarily, so I headed up to check out the room.

John R. Knuth

I opened the door to find a smallish, beautifully kept room. The paint was a pale yellow and the room was adorned with a TV and a mini refrigerator. The closet had a safe and a built-in organizer to lay out your shirts and pants. The bathroom was tiled in an orange and brown quarry tile with bottled water by the sink. A fresh fruit tray with two apples and a pear along with a bottle of Morande carmenere awaited me. In addition, a personalized welcome card, a hat and a polo shirt rounded out my goodies. Very nice. I plugged my PC in to charge and within a few seconds there was a knock on the door…my luggage as promised. This time I handed the guy three dollars and he advised me in his broken English to let him know if there was anything else he could do. I thanked him and he left. After a quick unpacking, it was my down time. I wanted to hit the gym for a light workout to stretch and get the blood flowing, so I quickly changed and headed downstairs. Dave was already down at the business center trying to get the e-mail going so I got my safe key and headed into the gym in the hotel. Again, very nice. A large area filled with free weights, circuit machines, treadmills, bikes, and so on was ours for the asking. A desk attendant followed me down to show me the area and grabbed a towel for me. I hit the weights for about a half hour, then Dave showed up. He soon was jogging on a treadmill and I joined him for 10 minutes at an easy pace. My legs felt tired and heavy. After that I headed upstairs to the "Business Center" where

My Chilean Wine Odyssey
A Week Touring the Wine Country of Chile

a PC was on-line for guest use. I proceeded to send my wife, Carmen, an e-mail letting her know I'd arrived safely and how much I missed her. I both sent and received mail under AT&T's web site, so I hoped communication would remain good with home. Afterwards I came back to the room for a shower and a brief rest. As I lay down to rest I felt I needed to keep my log going so I hit the computer. It showed 13:03 on the clock (curious how they use military time), letting me know I had a half an hour to get dressed and meet the others for lunch and our city tour. Jaime said to grab the cameras.

Chapter 4

Sunday, March 8, 2003

Lunch and beyond!

Off to lunch we went to a place two blocks from our hotel called "Happenings." A short walk on this glorious day had us at the restaurant within minutes. We were joined by three other members of the Morande team, Ximena (pronounced Hi Main A), who handled all the details of our arrangements in Chile, Juan Pablo, one of the original partners in Morande and Miguel Luis, public relations. We met at 1:45, early for Chilean lunch. We were escorted to an upstairs room in an upscale restaurant where we were introduced to the intricacies of the local drink of Chile, the pisco sour. Pisco is a local brew made from the Muscat grape, a notoriously sweet grape

My Chilean Wine Odyssey
A Week Touring the Wine Country of Chile

(think of muscatel) and then fermented into a brandy. Lime juice, a bit of egg whites and some bitters are added for a concoction which resembles a margarita. We all sat around the table, introduced ourselves, and the feast began. We started with bread, crackers and rolls served with butter, local salsa and green chilies and chopped onions. Next we indulged in a meat stuffed empanada. Our piscos were nearing empty so the Morande wines began to flow. Starting with reserve merlot, we moved into our salads, a lovely affair with mixed greens of all sorts and a light balsamic vinaigrette which was soft enough not to ruin our wine. The discussion around the table was mostly about the liquor/wine business. Good conversation continued as the sausages appeared. One was a cross between bratwurst and pepperoni if you can imagine such a creation. The other was a pork blood sausage with onion. That was a little too much for my unsophisticated palate. I had a few bites but had to pass on the rest. I learned that I wanted an agua sin gas, which meant a plain bottled water. An agua con gas would have been a fizzy type of affair which I just didn't care for. Several toasts later, which were very sincere from our friends at Morande, the reserve cabernet came out. Our main entrée was a sampling of two cuts of beef from Argentina. The first, a thick slab of beef, which reminded me of a New York strip steak, the second, a top butt. Both were *way* too rare for me. I politely asked for a bit more cooking, as others soon joined in my cry for non-bleeding beef. No problem as my steaks soon came back cooked to perfection. During this lengthy lunch, Juan Pablo indicated that a typical lunch on a weekend could be three hours long. It was the Chilean way of quality time and it was expected and enjoyed by the entire family. More toasts and more talk about wine and the liquor business continued. I managed to get a few photos of our group and our waiter. Agustin was polite and efficient. Dessert was a choice of a caramel latte thing or sliced apples served with a caramel sauce and vanilla ice cream. The table was split 50/50 on dessert as we continue to force the sweet stuff down. We knew we were heading out on a city tour after lunch so we tried to behave. Everyone seemed to have a fun time and was getting along very well. The hospitality of our Chilean hosts was unbelievable. We all quickly learned that the custom in Chile is that if you look at the bill when it comes, you are expected to pay. Needless to say, everyone minded their own business!

Juan Pablo gave his good byes (he had been sick all the previous week and wanted to get back home to rest) while we took a casual stroll back to the hotel. We were greeted by our bus driver Jose, and Abelardo, affectionately known as Abe, our tour guide for the day. Our bus tour took us up and down Providencia Avenue, the longest running street in Chile, which runs from the Andes all the way to the western side of Santiago. We started east and headed west. New Santiago is a very beautiful place, but the further west (and downhill, both literally and figuratively) we saw the old Santiago. Many beautiful buildings remained, once private residences of the rich and famous. These properties were taken over by the government during the Pinochet years. Interestingly enough, Jaime offered another perspective on the brutal dictator. He indicated that Pinochet had set up many programs and plans which helped the Chilean economy prosper since his departure. On a sad personal note, one of Jaime's relatives was a victim of the brutality, taking a one way voyage out to sea, which was a fairly common occurrence for dissidents. I took some pictures of private residence, which in their day must have been fantastic castles. Today, some are vacant while others are getting a new lease on life as university buildings and homes for business. The former residents have all moved on, either further east in Santiago or back to their home lands.

We toured the outside presidential palace, where giant doors of Oregon pine protected the entrances. Guards in pressed uniforms politely watched over the grounds. We also managed to stop at the local horse racing track, a beautiful facility despite our distant views of the grounds. Off to the mountain peak of St. Christobal where a concrete statue of the Virgin Mary stands guard over Santiago, reminiscent of Rio de Janeiro, Brazil's concrete

Christ. Hoards of locals walked around the dangerous drops without any signs of handrails or protective structures. Carmen would have been frantic with our kids around. A beautiful view, despite the cellular and electrical towers in the way. So is Santiago, the old and the new struggling to survive in harmony. The evening was beginning to set in so we headed back down the mountain and through more local neighborhoods onto a jewelry shop which specialized in the lapis lazuli, a semi-precious gemstone only found in Chile and Afghanistan. Obviously Afghanistan's market had taken a nose dive in recent years, so we perused the many beautiful items. Jaime said not to rush into a purchase as we would have several opportunities to view other works by local craftsmen, but the stuff we saw tonight was top notch. Mike (from Colorado) and I tried to negotiate a "bulk" discount for some stuff and to the surprise of Jaime managed to get a quote of 15% off invoice! We didn't buy but did take their cards. They offered to send a car to our hotel to bring us back if we so desired.

As we approached our hotel the time was nearing 8:00 pm. Ximena bade us farewell for the evening as we went back into our hotel ready to dine again. This time it was to be a casual affair in the hotel restaurant featuring real Chilean sea bass. Everyone was getting tired so we all agreed to do a quick room stop and meet in the restaurant bar for a drink before

My Chilean Wine Odyssey
A Week Touring the Wine Country of Chile

dinner. An ice cold glass and a bottle of Kuntzman Pale Ale was my drink of choice, a German style brew from the south of the country which reminded me of a Spaten. We sat around the bar for a few minutes while everyone's eyes began to glaze over. We were all exhausted so we chose to eat before we began to fall asleep. Once again Morande wines were waiting for us at the table and a fresh salad with apples (to offset the vinegar to make our wine taste better!). The sea bass made its way out on a bed of Italian seasoned gnocchi and some local greens. The combination was out of this world. I managed to eat all of my sea bass and most of the gnocchi. A brief discussion pursued about the truth or myth of the declining populations of the Chilean sea bass. Jaime is a firm believer that it is far from the truth and just the local environmentalist taking issue. Regardless, it was good. A dessert followed and everyone seemed to groan but managed to have a few bites. Dave and Jim had a discussion about a web site Jim had visited and found a phone card deal offering rates from Chile for 30 cents a minute. Dave excused himself and went to make a phone call. We all laughed and talked for a few more minutes and decided it was time to call it a day. Jaime advised us that we had another full day ahead of us, to take in breakfast between 6:30 and 9:00 and be ready for a full day of wine presentations and marketing. I said my goodbyes and headed up to the business center to send a few e-mails. E-mail is a very convenient way to communicate. I miss everyone, but feel able to communicate rather seamlessly with e-mail access. I wasn't able to send pictures like I had hoped, but continued to take advantage of my new digital camera and shot lots of pictures. I had been categorizing the pictures by date. My plans were to finish this document and work the photos into it to help tell the story. I promised the others in the group that I would forward a disk of the pictures to each of the them. They all seemed like good people, and I have enjoyed the business talk. I had been typing for about an hour and it was after 11:00. I was tired yet very satisfied with things so far. I was looking forward to the next few days.

Chapter 5

Monday, March 10, 2003

Wine 101

A good night's sleep…a rare thing for me. I awoke only once during the evening and quickly fell back to sleep. At 6:30 local time, I woke up and pondered where I was. I was not at all scared or lonely and thought "I could easily live in this country." I finally got out of bed at 7:00 and got dressed for a light workout. Dave was downstairs looking for a running partner, but I chose to stay in. Off he went. I checked my e-mails and discovered a friendly "Thanks for sending me an update" letter from Donna, my neighbor. I sent a few quick notes to some friends and headed for the gym. The PC in the lobby really gave me a sense of being connected. You could knock out an e-mail in a minute or two and read someone's response minutes later.

The gym this morning was quite different than yesterday afternoon, which only makes sense. Monday, everyone was off to business meetings and the morning gym had at least 15, 35 - 50 years old I guessed. I chose to row for 10 minutes and ride a bike for 25 more minutes. All four TV's were on Spanish TV, two on CNN, one on MTV and one on ESPN (Spanish equivalents). No one seemed to mind me, but a section came on about Iraq and the conversation quickly blossomed amongst the men. It seemed light hearted, but somehow I was thankful I didn't understand what they were saying. I kept pedaling and the story soon changed. After my workout, I headed up for a shower. Monday was scheduled to be a working day so I put on some khaki pants and a polo shirt. I was comfortable in my room and getting dressed at a leisurely pace was fun. Down I went for breakfast where Dave was on the PC. He indicated he took a little longer jog than he wanted, losing direction for a bit. He was busy sending his family e-mail, so I headed down to the hotel restaurant where several others were already sitting. I chose a glass of orange juice and a chirimoya, a very sweet juice which reminded me of pear nectar, a roll with some fried ham and fresh fruit and a cup of coffee. It hit the spot. The table conversation was mostly about the agenda for the day, local foods and how tired everyone was last night. Dave joined us several minutes later and we continued on for a few more minutes. It was almost 9:00 and our meeting was scheduled for 10:00. I decided to head out and walk for a while. It was a beautiful morning, 80 degrees and sunny. I knew Providencia Boulevard was only two blocks south, so I headed there. It was the main thoroughfare so I knew I couldn't get lost. Santiago was busy going to work. It seemed to be a little slower and easier pace than we have back home. As I passed people, I noticed no one seemed to exchange greetings, but kept their faces looking forward and headed on to wherever they were going. I gave an occasional buenos dias to the street workers who all seemed happy that someone noticed them. Jaime has indicated that the Chilean people are shy by nature. If you were to say good morning in an elevator, you might get a strange look or two. I don't believe the population was unfriendly, just kind of quiet.

After a ten block walk I decided to head back. I noticed a handicapped man under the shade of a tree in the parkway shining shoes. I asked how much and he said something back I didn't understand. I had $5 in my pocket and figured that would cover it and sat down. It was wonderful watching people come and go. I didn't understand my shoe shiner's name, but I asked him for his photo as I left. He gladly agreed so I snapped a picture. He did a nice job on my shoes too! I'd often heard the travel guy on Channel 11, Rick Steves, suggest the best way to take in a foreign country was to do stuff the local people did. For me it was 10 minutes of pure pleasure. Sounds silly that sitting in a chair and having someone shine your shoes could possibly be that much fun, but I was exploring on my own, at my pace and on my terms. I stopped in a local drug store to buy some toothpaste. It seemed I accidentally packed one of my kid's toothpaste and was getting kind of tired of the bubble gum flavor. I was surprised to see a lack of local brands in the store. Most everything I saw was the familiar Crest, Colgate, etc. Oh well, I kind of like bubble gum anyway! I headed back for my meeting and called it quits for my morning sightseeing.

We had a half hour break from our first presentation. We were a little late getting going, but the presentation focused on the structure of Morande, their marketing strategy, as well as an overview of the brief history of the wine business, particularly the wine export history of Chile. A bit tedious at times and not unlike so many presentations we have all been to, but what really captured my attention was the passion these guys had. They continually insist that passion is required in the wine business and you can tell they believe it. Juan Pablo Barrios was doing most of the talking this morning. His English was very good, but he had a *thick* accent. He managed

My Chilean Wine Odyssey
A Week Touring the Wine Country of Chile

to successfully get his point across and two hours later we were given a half hour break. Our next segment would focus primarily on international wine consumption trends. Not bad. After all, this is why we came.

We had a fifteen minute break to have some coffee and walk a bit. Checked my e-mails and had some fresh squeezed orange juice. The afternoon segment of the presentation was a review of current statistics on world-wide wine consumption patterns. Actually it was quite interesting, showing which types of grapes are being planted where, who's gaining ground in the import/export world, overall wine consumption vs. beer. So on and so forth. Jaime did a good job of making the entire thing quite interesting. Not too much interaction with the guys, but I think I learned a lot. We were all promised a copy of the entire presentation on CD before we left. We broke for a lunch at 1:30 and were told to meet back in the lobby in five minutes. Everyone scrambled up to their rooms for a bathroom break, to grab some money and get their cameras.

Lunch stop was at a place called Pimpilinpausha, a nice looking place with a large open-air front patio. The former Chilean ambassador to France was having lunch with his gang. Juan Pablo knew him, but didn't seem too impressed with him. Our group once again had a semi-private room towards the back. Our waitress, Nora, quickly asked for our afternoon cocktail. I chose another Chilean specialty, a Vaina, port wine mixed with egg white and a touch of cinnamon sprinkled on top. Very good, but a tad sweet. Piscos were also being passed around. Our conversation was pretty light while dinner orders were being taken. Our first course was an appetizer for which I chose red peppers stuffed with ground meat, served in a sauce of tomato, onion and olive oil. Morande pinot noir and merlot were promptly poured into our glasses. I started with the pinot noir, which wasn't quite enough wine for the slightly spicy appetizer, so I had to start on the merlot. A nice complement. Carmen would have liked it. Next was a choice of entrees. Our choices included filet mignon, with either mushrooms or port wine sauce, shrimp risotto or marluza, a local fish. The marluza would be served with olives, tomatoes and onions. The fish was my choice and it was excellent. The pinot noir was a natural selection with spicy olives and tomatoes. I could get used to this very easily, but then came dessert. A cappuccino would compliment my lucuma cake. Lucuma is a tropical fruit which is very sweet. It looks something like passion fruit, with an orange flesh, like a pumpkin and a large seed in the middle, also something like an avocado. Regardless of the strange configuration, the cake was very light and very sweet, having an almost dry, flaky sugar consistency. Time was once again slipping away from us as it was nearing 4:00. We headed out, thanking everyone for a great lunch, to check out some local wine shops and a grocery store.

The first wine store was right across the street from our restaurant. A gorgeous 85 degrees day with no humidity greeted us as we donned our sun glasses. The wine shop was a sight to behold. "El Mundo Del Vino" would make any retailer proud. Rows upon rows of beautifully crafted wood shelves cradled wines from around the world. We checked out the various offerings and after 20 minutes of "oohing and aahing" headed down the street for the next shop. The second shop, while not quite as impressive as the first, again was loaded with fine wines, featuring a more limited world-wide selection. However, Chile was well represented. I started looking for souvenirs and Jaime reminded me we would be stopping at the Morande store, which I would chose as my shop for most of my wine related gifts.

Our next stop was at the local mall...and what a mall it was. The mall was very large, occupying three floors. Even though we were half way around the world, the place had a familiar feel to it. I guess a mall is a mall regardless of where you go. Mothers dragging their kids, high school kids hanging out, seniors walking around looking a little overwhelmed, you know...a typical mall. Jumbo was the grocery store we were going to stop in, but to call it a grocery store would be doing it a grave injustice. The store made Wal-Mart appear small. I would even have to say it handily beat out the local Meijers as far as square footage goes. We all agreed to meet in the front of the store within a half and hour and Dave and I took off to explore the grocery store. It was quite impressive with a large produce section, fresh meats (maybe a little fresher than some would like) and aisles upon aisles of food. The store was quite huge. Both Dave and I wanted to get our daughters a CD of a "Michelle Branch" of Chile. I thought Jill would appreciate the CD and some earrings. After 3 or 4 attempts of communicating with local 12 year olds, we felt we better move on or risk getting arrested or worse, beaten by a concerned mother. We'd wait for a suggestion from Jaime. We ran into the others in, of course, the liquor section. Jaime was quite proud as his products were prominently displayed throughout the sections. I picked up the necessary supplies to treat my friends to homemade pisco sours. A bottle of 35 proof pisco and some sugar juice. The recipe is for four parts pisco, one part sugar juice and one part lime juice. Toss in a little egg white to give it some froth and blend it up. Sprinkle on a shot of bitters and call it a pisco sour. I am sure it wouldn't taste anything like what we drank here, but what the heck, it would be fun. I exchanged a little currency so I could buy a few souvenirs. We headed for the mall as I wanted to get my son, Daniel, a soccer jersey from the Chilean

My Chilean Wine Odyssey
A Week Touring the Wine Country of Chile

team, Colo Colo. A little looking and we soon found it. $40.00 later on my credit card and we were heading back to the hotel. We were back by 7:00 and were told that this evening's dinner would be at Bali Hai. We were instructed to dress casually, bring our cameras, and be ready to go by 8:30; so off to the rooms we all scattered like cockroaches when the lights turn on. I think most everyone wanted to catch a few winks before the big night. I chose instead to keep typing. I knew I wouldn't regret my decision in the long run, but a 15 minute nap probably wouldn't have hurt. Bali Hai was promised to be a local tourist place with audience participation, etc. Jaime was convinced we would all have a lot of fun. I was sure he was right.

I finally got it. Tonight was a very fun night, but more importantly to me was that I finally got to see what Morande was all about. My respect for Jaime and Juan Pablo continued to grow each day. They were everything in people that one could ever want. More on Jaime and Juan Pablo after the details of the evening. After an hour or so of down time, our group met in the lobby for the usual pre-event talk time. We had all jelled very well as a group and were getting to know each other well. What was amazing to me is how well we fit together. Jaime was the ringleader...keeping things going, but I can say I actually liked these guys. Mike, our Colorado Italian, Jim, his quieter counter-part. Then the boys from Atlanta, Bruce and Dave. Don

John R. Knuth

from New Mexico and Tom from Connecticut. Dave and I, the boys from Chicago rounded out the group and we somehow or other seemed to fit together…well. But anyway, tonight we were meeting outside in our casual gear and Jaime appeared in khaki pants, a pink striped oxford shirt and a blue sport coat. Quite dapper. We got on the bus and headed out for dinner. We talked about tomorrow's agenda briefly and headed for the restaurant, Bali Hai. We arrived about 20 minutes later after a drive through central Santiago. The restaurant was as you may have expected, done in a Polynesian style. Slightly tacky, but it worked. Our group was one of the first to be seated, and the Morande guys once again came through as we had the best seats in the house. A menu was already printed especially for our group, complete with the Morande logo. An opening cocktail, with choices ranging from the now famous pisco sours, Vaina, Maracuya (papaya) sours, rum punches and more. I think everyone chose a pisco sour, after all, we were getting to like them. At the recommendation of Juan Pablo and Jaime, I ordered the carpaccio, thinly sliced raw beef covered in lemon juice, onions, capers and balsamic vinegar. My main course was salmon and a papaya dessert. We'd had other choices, but I followed the advice of my new friends and was promised I wouldn't be disappointed, and I wasn't. I had never relished the thought of raw beef, but this was something entirely different. It seemed as though the citrus juice had actually cooked the stuff

My Chilean Wine Odyssey
A Week Touring the Wine Country of Chile

to a medium-well consistency. I ate it all (except a small bite I gave to Dave) and enjoyed it immensely. Our wines for the evening were again Morande, carmenere and chardonnay. The carmenere was a natural choice for the beef. I had already finished my pisco as the wine began to pour. Soon, a wonderful cut of salmon fillet was brought, covered in a light herb sauce. Chardonnay was perfect. I was purring like a kitten, entirely happy with my food choices. Salmon hasn't always been a favorite of mine, but due to the freshness of the fish, the wine, the piscos or the ambience, it was great. Our waiter, a slight fellow named Victor, took good care of us. We were joined this evening by Marcelo, a gentleman from Argentina who spoke a broken, but intelligible English, and Luis Matte, the CEO of Morande. They seemed to fit into our group seamlessly. It was almost 11:00 when we finished our food and the floor show began.

It would be difficult to not compare the show with a cross between a Saturday Night Live skit featuring Bill Murray and the Disney film "Three Caballeros." A music tribute to all of the countries of South America done by a live band and a lounge singer followed. It was hard not to join in despite not understanding the language. Jaime admitted he was an accomplished singer and his bellowing voice accompanied every Latin song our host belted out. I was really getting to like this guy. The host continued around the room asking people where they were from and sang a song from their country. When he got to us, the chosen song was "When the Saints Go Marching In." Not my first choice, but by then I really didn't care. I needed to go to the bathroom but Jaime insisted I stay as the Polynesian review was about to start. By now I was getting to know Jaime well enough to figure out that some type of audience participation was about to happen. Bruce and Dave were the intended targets…and I believed him. Soon the dancers headed out in the audience and I too was chosen. I didn't argue but went with it. One by one we did our little jungle dance. When it came to Dave, he did it up right. They unbuttoned his shirt and the dancing began. You have to understand that Chile is a conservative country. Nowhere had we seen any signs of sexuality, and even in this show, everything, and I mean everything was clean cut. The shirt scene was very tastefully done and Dave gave it his best. He played along well and danced his heart out. Everyone was proud of him and we all clapped as loud as we could and snapped dozens of pictures. Soon the show was over and the band played Latin dance music. Jaime asked Ximena to dance and the two of them hit the dance floor alone. Both of them were accomplished dancers. Jaime had his perennial smile on his face and Ximena was right there with him. It was enchanting listening to the beat of the music watching these two dance. For a moment I became quite jealous of Jaime. He was handsome, dressed smartly, could sing and dance, speak many languages, was wittier than most (especially me!), likeable and had that smile glued to his face...and he liked his job and everyone around him! Then I noticed Ximena, she too was magical to watch. Never sexual, never flirtatious, the two of them danced their Latin tango with style. While the two of them danced, we all sat and watched. Juan Pablo was directly across from me and I noticed he, too, had a huge smile on.

It hit me. I had gotten it. I had figured out Morande. Today, in our first meeting, Juan Pablo went out of his way to discuss his company's values with everyone. I don't remember every single item on the list, but things like honesty, friendship, flexibility and relationships were all on the list. The people of Morande are truly the best of the best. They lived and worked their lives with passion, a different passion than we as Americans understand. We can have fun, but these people <u>are</u> fun, a big difference. Jaime, Juan Pablo, Ximena, Miguel and Luis all are PMA (positive mental attitude), have great personalities, are hospitable Chileans and smart, suave individuals...the best of the best. They believe it and they live it. I kind of had my Chilean moment then. The expense of having us as guests for a week suddenly seemed to make perfect sense. They needed this time to show us who and what they were, and watching Jaime and Ximena dancing their Latin tango had made it hit home. The "glow" factor really hit me. My moment had come and suddenly, for a brief period of time, the world became a different place. The feeling of my American superiority quickly wilted to these wonderful people. It must sound incredibly hokey, but it was very real to me. I would learn a lot from these guys. First Dave, then Jim, took Jaime's turns dancing with Ximena. One by one she showed them the right steps to look good on the dance floor. An excellent dancer, she had everyone smiling. No sexuality, just pure style and class. I am afraid that in the states someone would have suggested taking eight guys to a strip club or a gentlemen's club. But this was a class event, kind of like watching a Jay Leno comedy routine, no swearing, but you still laugh. Hats off to Morande, I got it.

Tomorrow would be a big day so Jaime called everyone's attention to the time and we all headed out to the bus. All were smiling and laughing as we headed back home. Many pictures and images would remain forever, but for me I would always remember the night as the night the Morande vision jelled.

When I got back to the hotel, I checked my e-mail. Sure enough, each of my kids had sent a letter letting me know how much they missed me. I went to bed at 1:00 am feeling quite emotional. Having made such good new friends and missing my family, I was overtired and needed to get some sleep.

Chapter 6

Tuesday, March 11, 2003

The Vineyards and Pablo

An early rise and it was time to get moving. Jaime was serious about being ready by 8:30 am, not that we had ever been late. I went to the gym early this morning and it was still dark. I managed to turn on a treadmill and walked for 15 or so minutes before the attendant came in. We exchanged "holas" and the lights came on. Another 15 minutes of exercise, which felt like torture, made me wish I'd stayed in bed. Off for breakfast and our first trip to the vineyards of Pelequen to see the grapes and the winery.

My Chilean Wine Odyssey
A Week Touring the Wine Country of Chile

I met up with Don, Jaime and Tom for breakfast this morning. Before Tom and Jaime arrived, I discussed with Don some of my feelings about Morande and their passion. Don was in full agreement with me so I knew it was more than alcohol I had been feeling the previous night. Whew!

The breakfast buffet had a new fruit out this morning. It looked somewhat like a kiwi, but with larger and more colorful seeds. We suspected this was a tuna, a local fruit that is also called a cactus fruit. Don, quite fluent in espanol, asked a waiter who confirmed our suspicions. We both ate up, and it was good…somewhat of a mix between a kiwi and a honeydew melon. A roll with some ham and some fresh juice and I wandered back to the room to get ready. We were all going to wear our complimentary Morande shirts today. They were black, and it's promised to be hot. I was sure we'd be warm in the vineyards, but at least we'd look good.

Jaime shed a little light on his name. His business card is printed with Jaime Merino C. The C stood for his mother's maiden name, Castro. Her brother was Raul Castro, an officer in the navy with a name the same as another famous Castro. (When a woman gets married, she keeps her name plus his. Now I knew.)

At 7:15 pm, I was back in my hotel room. Quite a bit had happened this afternoon and I felt if I didn't spend some time putting it down, I'd quickly forget as each event continued to be more grand than the next. Our group was scheduled for a formal dinner this evening with the Board of Directors of Morande. The plan was to meet in the lobby by 8:30. A nap sounded good, but there were just too many things to remember, so back I went to my computer.

Our trip this morning had started out in our tour bus (a very comfortable affair which held 25, allowing our group of 9 or 10 a lot of space) heading down the side streets of Santiago towards the town of Pelequen. The winery was located outside of town, but before we went to the winery, we were to first stop at a vineyard owned by Morande where Macarena Morande, Pablo's daughter, managed the vineyard. The ride out of town was bumpy as we worked our way through side streets. Santiago suffers from a lack of planning for the phenomenal growth which had occurred there in the last several decades. Very few dedicated thoroughfares exist so often times the side streets are the only way to go. As we weaved our way through town, we got to see more of Santiago, some of the beautiful and some of the not so beautiful. Like any major city, there were poor sections, however, they

My Chilean Wine Odyssey
A Week Touring the Wine Country of Chile

didn't seem necessarily unsafe, but clearly lacking compared to where we were staying. Many city projects were going on and I'd, say very few, if any, heavy equipment helped out with the intensive manual labor. Trenches and earthmoving were done by groups of three or four men, all working shovels to place utilities, pipes, or whatever it was they were doing. It seemed to take quite a while to get out of town, but soon we were motoring our way South on the famous Pan American highway. Unlike the expressways in America which don't allow slower moving vehicles, life on this interstate was obviously quite different. People walking and riding bikes were everywhere. Groups of local vendors selling things such as soda, fruits, vegetables and whatever else were busy catering to their traveling customers. They appeared a bit more rustic than I would probably want, but the locals obviously had a different opinion.

The bus rumbled down the highway for another 30 minutes or so and vineyards began to appear along the roadside. The lush green canopies of the vineyard painted a vibrant foreground to the dull rock covered mountains looming directly behind. The sun painted its morning light on the entire scene and it was beautiful. The bus slowed and we made an exit, directly from the busy highway, onto a clay and gravel road. Several hundred yards down this rustic road were a handful of small buildings, obviously serving as the offices for the vineyard. The bus slowly pulled ahead onto the rough path and we saw Ximena and another younger woman ahead of us. Jaime had advised us that Pablo Morande's daughter, Macarena, would be there to greet us. Macarena was in her mid-to-late 20's. She was wearing an apricot polo shirt, jeans and tennis shoes. No make-up found its way onto her beautiful face and she had the appearance of a farm girl on her home turf. She was quite informal as we were introduced to her one by one. We began walking into the neatly planted rows of grapes while given a lesson in vineyard management. Macarena had obviously grown up in the family business as she was very "into" the many nuances and minute details of managing a vineyard. This particular vineyard was located in the Maipe valley and produces some of the finest grapes used by Morande. Berries from this vineyard make it into Morande's Limited Edition wines and it was pretty clear that Macarena was one of the reasons for this. She began to produce aerial photos of the roughly 120 acres. Colored charts indicating soil composition, moisture retention, rock composition, soil depths, so on and so on, were all part of her arsenal to produce as fine a berry as possible. Macarena was also proud of how well she knew every foot of the vineyard and indicated several sectors of the vineyard which produced excellent grapes. The group was invited and encouraged to walk down the rows and taste the grapes, which were nearly ready for harvest.

Carmenere, then merlot, a cabernet franc...the vines were loaded with berries. The berries were smaller and sweeter than I had expected compared with varieties we see in our stores. Irrigation is withheld as the berries form in order to keep cell size small and produce more intensely-flavored berries. Juan Pablo joined the group as we continued our way down the rows and soon needed to head onto the winery, still an hour or so drive away. The bus was once again loaded and we bade farewell to Macarena.

Back on the bus, we continued south on the Pan American highway. The highway seemed to be unable to go more than several miles without large sections under repair, necessitating high speed veers to the right and then back to the left...at least they were using heavy machinery here. Kilometer after kilometer we headed further from Santiago, passing some shanty towns, small neighborhoods, vineyards, commercial fruit companies and highway under construction, all with the Andes mountains looming in the background. My eyes grew tired and I drifted in and out of a light sleep, not wanting to miss anything, yet very tired with the hot sun shining on me. Life here seemed much simpler.

Vina Morande appeared as a dozen or so newly constructed metal buildings with a handsome iron corporate seal in the front lawn. Security guards swung open huge metal gates as we made our way to the front doors of the reception area into the gravel parking lot. One by one we unloaded and stood in the now hot fall sun and waited for Pablo to join us. A few moments later a man clad in blue jeans and a blue Morande polo shirt walked around the corner talking with someone. Having seen pictures of the man, I knew it was Pablo. He shook everyone's hands in a reserved fashion and it was now his show. Jaime and Juan Pablo both let Pablo Morande take over as this was his place of business. Our crowd, or at least Dave and I, seemed intimidated by this man who had traveled the world making Chile known in the wine business. His English was quite good, but he seemed a man of few words. We were escorted into a newly constructed reception area and moved into the "tasting room." Here nine glasses of wine had been carefully poured; there was a water glass, napkins, crackers and a spittoon. This was going to be a serious tasting. We all scurried around the table and jockeyed for a spot. I didn't want to get too close to Pablo as I was honestly afraid of my lack of knowledge. Waiting for Pablo, he sat, then we did. Wine tasting sheets were distributed and the place got darn right quiet. The Master sat there controlling the pace while we waited. I nervously worked my way through several wines, not wanting to say anything which revealed how little I actually knew. Pablo didn't seem to care, but I did. The wines were all very good, but I can honestly say my mind wasn't as concerned with the wines as it was about doing, or not doing, something wrong. Ximena and another younger male employee were on my left, Dave to the right. Ximena commented on the need to be quiet so we could concentrate...I think she was a little intimidated too!

One by one we worked our way through the wines. Jaime finally offered some comic relief to get the conversation going. It worked. Pablo warmed up, things began to loosen up and it looked as if we made it through. The wines were good, and that was the message Morande wanted to get across. It was fun to hear the words of the creator, the artist. It was his vision and drive that created what was in front of us, and he was obviously proud of the end product. Macarena joined us for the tasting of the wine she had created, an chardonnay ice wine that she invented while she did an internship at the world famous Opus One winery in California. The teacher beamed as his student explained her wine. The joy of parenthood crosses all cultures as the proud father envisioned the day the student would become the teacher. The mood was much lighter as we finished up and began to move around. Pablo was the clear leader, but Jaime remained the jokester, keeping the mood light. It was time for our tour of the wine-making facilities. The tour started outside where various species of grapes were grown, to demonstrate the berry size, leaf size, vine structure and so on. We tried more varieties of grapes, some of which I'd never heard of before. Each different, each better in the shade, each better on the west side of the vine...wine making is complicated.

The wine making facilities were pretty much as I'd expected. I'd read enough literature on the wine making process that I recognized most of the apparatus. What struck me was the amount of infrastructure needed to make the operation work. Luis latter confirmed the amount was approximately ten million US dollars for physical assets, another ten million in wine inventory (the stuff has to age - remember) and five million dollars in working capital...and he still feels broke all the time. It sounds familiar. Crushers, de-stemmers, barrels, and tons of stainless steel all neatly arranged and very clean. As the operation is a new, ground-up facility, it was designed around a smooth flow of material, which according to Pablo, was somewhat of a luxury as many older vineyards have added pieces here and there to keep up with demand, which leads to some less than desirable physical property arrangements. The tour was interrupted by several phone calls and people coming up to Pablo, something was up that we wouldn't find out about till later that evening. Suddenly Jaime was our tour guide as we wrapped things up, which was okay as we were all getting a bit tired and it was almost 3:00. We gave our thanks to the people at the winery and headed off to lunch.

Chapter 7

Tuesday, March 11, 2003

Lunch at Hacienda Los Lingues

Our group once again was in the bus, now noticeably quieter as we headed somewhere unknown for lunch. The scenery kept us occupied while Jaime, Miguel and Jose debated on how to get where we were going…we were obviously lost, at least a little. A few minutes and a few U-turns later we turned off the highway onto a much coarser road leading off into nowhere. It wasn't too long before the semi-paved road turned into a clay and dirt road. Where we were headed was a mystery to me. My front seat perch in the bus let me see how far off the beaten path we were going. Soon, we came head to head with a steamroller on a deserted section of road 3 or 4 kilometers from the highway. The steamroller gladly moved off the shoulder of soft dirt and we plodded along towards our un-charted destination. Vineyards soon appeared on both sides of the road and the bus passed an entrance gate. The grounds instantly became immaculate gardens of pampered plants, while a few dogs, obvious residents of the fine property, ran out to greet us. The bus pulled around a circular drive and the intrepid travelers all left the bus somewhat awestruck by the beautifully manicured surroundings. Jaime and Miguel exchanged some greetings with a staff member who came out to greet us. A motion was made to follow and we soon were on a concreted-edged gravel path along beautiful gardens. Several large buildings loomed to our left, but our destination was elsewhere. A clearing soon appeared and five tables were lined up in the shade. Colorful linens graced each table and it was obvious that this was where lunch was being served. It was out of a dream…a colorful setting that would match any four star restaurant in a travel book. It was so tranquil that you were very aware of the peace and silence. Oohs and aahs quickly followed as we pulled up chairs. It was lots of fun being treated so well. The sun shone through the trees, the temperature was 80 to 85 degrees, zero humidity and a gentle breeze. It was heaven.

My Chilean Wine Odyssey
A Week Touring the Wine Country of Chile

Hacienda Los Lingues was a place that had to be seen to be believed. Don't come here expecting a large swimming pool with a swim up bar. This place is all about peace and tranquility. If you want to check the place out, they have a website; www.loslingues.cl. The wait staff quickly swarmed our tables offering water and pouring…Morande wines. This time sauvignon blanc, merlot and pinot noir were soon swirling around our bottomless glasses. Warm rolls were passed around and once again I found myself dining. It was almost 3:30 and we knew we had a long day still ahead of us, but lunch isn't rushed in Chile. An empanada filled with ground beef, olives and onion was next. I was hungry and it tasted good! Wines and laughter filled the quiet, peaceful late afternoon air. A hammock was strung between two tree branches and it seemed to call to me. A few pictures later and I reluctantly returned to our lunchtime feast. Two resident dogs gently tried to persuade "treats," but didn't get very far as they were shooed from guest to guest. A salad of tomato, onions and herbs served with a shepherd's pie, filled with ground beef, chicken and topped with a polenta, rounded out the menu, especially for me. Finally, a fruit salad containing both yellow and white peaches, melon and tuna was presented. Thank goodness that was all, a relatively light lunch for Vina Morande, but it was perfect. Coffee, then a tour of the grounds followed. The hacienda was built in the 1500's and was still owned by the same family. Inside, ornate antiques, hand-carved woods, glorious wood armoires, Queen Anne furniture, hardwood floors, tiles, and more filled each room. Time was once again running late as it was 5:00 and we had a two to three hour ride back into Santiago. We couldn't afford to be late as tonight was our formal dinner with the Board of Directors of Morande.

The bus headed back on its bouncy and desolate journey to the highway. Jaime announced he was officially off duty for the next couple of hours and that a nap may be a good idea. Within minutes the bus was quiet as people either drifted off looking out the windows or quickly fell asleep. I did the latter and awoke arriving into Santiago. Our path in seemed to go quicker than the way out despite heavy traffic. School and work were getting out and it was almost 7:00 pm. We pulled into the hotel and were given instructions to be ready to go by 8:40 in the lobby. This gave me time to keep my journal up to date, and I had lots to write about. Today was another full day. 45 minutes of typing became my first casualty to not saving data every few minutes. I must have hit *Control X* by mistake and lost everything I had just entered. I had once again been reminded for the need to save my work. I won't allow that to happen again as *Control S* had been burnt into my memory. The next 30 minutes were spent trying to remember My typing catastrophe ended up making me late for dinner. I jumped into the shower and quickly got dressed. Tonight was our formal dinner and it required our suit jackets. It felt good getting dressed up as I put on my suit coat. I became very aware of my aloneness as I once again wished Carmen had come along with me. I continued rushing to get out of the room and closed the door at 8:35, camera and notepad in hand, as we were off to dinner…again.

Chapter 8

Tuesday, March 11, 2003

Dinner with the Board

Once again our tour bus was off to a destination unknown. Jose, quite impressed with the group in our suits, made comments to us all. Off we went through downtown Santiago. Weather continued to be beautiful as the bus headed to a restaurant we were told is owned by a couple from Peru. The restaurant was a first in Santiago as it had an open kitchen format. No one seemed very hungry, but we were all excited about the big dinner. We knew Pablo would be there, along with Luis and Juan Pablo, but after that we were unsure about the rest.

My Chilean Wine Odyssey
A Week Touring the Wine Country of Chile

One thing that makes Santiago such an approachable city may be its seeming lack of zoning. Hotels and restaurants are sprinkled through the small side streets. Business and apartments often share a same block. This gives Santiago a small town feeling, even though it has almost six million residents. Astrid and Gaston's restaurant was bustling with a large Tuesday night crowd. The place was classy looking from the street and with Morande's track record to date, a disappointment was very improbable. And disappointed we weren't. The restaurant was a modern affair with beautiful wood and wine everywhere. Our private dining room had doors which were held open as the evening was gorgeous. All parties were well dressed as we met familiar faces and several new ones. The banker, Carlos Spoerer, a handsome Chilean (whose wife is from LaPorte, Indiana!) and Carlos Mackenna, the new CEO of the Morande, Chile. Apparently all the commotion at the winery was a restructuring, and Luis Matte was now the international CEO, while a new manager of daily operations was hired to take care of day to day operations in Chile. Luis would be focusing on international growth. We gathered around the table and found seats and sat down. Numerous toasts were given and once again, Morande wines made their way out. A pre-printed menu for the evening was wrapped with a gold ribbon, written in Spanish. Our appetizer was a choice of scallops served in sauce with caviar or salmon served with some herbal dressing. The main entrée was a tough one, Chilean sea bass, done with stuff and more stuff, or a filet, served with garlic potatoes. Dessert? I didn't think I would care so I did not bother to pay attention while Jaime translated the offerings. The wines for the evening would all be Morande Limited Edition, first chardonnay, then cabernet franc and then late harvest sauvignon blanc. I knew from our tasting this morning that the cabernet franc was perfect for the fillet, plus I had already had eaten sea bass. Scallops were the choice for my appetizer as I had a salmon fillet the night before, and the salmon would be a lot of fish for the chardonnay. I made my decisions, and was given a "good choice" by Pablo, who was sitting directly across from me. He ordered the same. I gave the waiter the okay to choose a dessert for me, not that it would matter because I would eat whatever they sent.

Our scallops arrived, served in the shell. The chardonnay was poured and the combination was excellent. Conversations struck up between individuals sitting by each other. I had Jaime on my left and Luis on my right. I began speaking with Luis, about motorcycles, children (he has 5, 3 boys and 2 girls aged 12 to an infant, he's only 37). Wine, management, travel, the US, Chile, so on and so forth. I had the feeling if I lived here Luis and Juan Pablo would be friends of mine. They like to work, but also had personal interests similar to mine, and kids whose ages closely matched mine as well.

The fillet was brought out next and we watched Pablo taste the new cabernet franc and nod to the waiter that it met with his satisfaction. Our glasses were soon full, and never had an opportunity to go below 1/3 full. The fillet and potatoes were excellent, prepared perfectly medium-well done as I had ordered. The mood was light and occasional toasts were exchanged acknowledging new friendships.

The waiter brought my dessert, an assorted collection of tasty treats covered in a pile of sugar "hair." Jaime asked if I'd had brought my comb. It too was excellent. A round table discussion was initiated by Luis Matte about Morande and their work in the US. It went around the room as we discussed strategy, things which have worked and things which needed improvement. I enjoyed the conversation and believed it helped having the retailers point of view present at the meeting. It was getting late and everyone was tired. Pablo finally gave a quiet "time to leave" and everyone began to give their good byes.

John R. Knuth

Once again Morande had outdone themselves. We began our day touring a vineyard, then moved to the winery, enjoyed a private tasting, ate lunch in a place out of "Lifestyles", had a dinner meeting which was both fun and delicious, another wonderful day in Santiago. Jaime briefed us as we headed back to our hotel on the plans for tomorrow, check-out by 9:30 am, a quick tour of the Santiago office of Morande, on to the Casablanca valley for lunch, then on to Vina del Mar. I had to keep typing or I would have forgotten all the wonderful details.

Chapter 9

Wednesday, March 12, 2003

Casablanca Valley and Beyond

I was sleepy getting up. I wanted to hit the gym one last time, but it wasn't to be. I rolled myself out of bed at 7:00 and took a quick shower. Heading to the restaurant, I saw Dave on the veranda working on his PC. I grabbed a roll and some fresh fruit and looked for a waiter to get me some coffee. Dave was way ahead of me, already packed and ready to go. I finished my breakfast and headed up to the room to pack. Making sure I didn't leave anything, the usual paranoia of leaving something behind, where is all this stuff coming from, etc., you've done it all and this time wasn't any different. I was soon ready to go and gave a final check.

Checking out of the hotel was relatively painless, I returned my safe key and room keys, had to pay $3.00 for my mini-bar bill (a bottle of water) and waited for the rest of the guys to come down. We loaded the bus by 9:30 and we were off.

The Santiago office for Morande was your typical office in any town. Everyone was busy doing their normal Wednesday morning stuff. Marketing department, the technical support dept., accounting, and so on. It was nice for the broker guys as they got to put some faces to names. A whirlwind tour ended in Juan Pablo and Pablo Morande's offices and we were off.

The bus ride out of Santiago was on the section of highway where people travel from Santiago to Vina del Mar directly through the Casablanca valley. Vina del Mar is kind of a Monte Carlo of Chile and therefore the road is traveled by the well-heeled upper class of Santiago. Pablo Morande is credited for "discovering" the wonderful wine growing characteristics of this valley which is located only 45 minutes from the ocean. Our bus ride was uneventful, maybe even more so than usual in that the road we traveled on was in the best shape of any highway we had been on to date. As we went through a second tunnel, Jaime took the microphone and let us know that when we came out the other side we would be in the Casablanca valley. Once the bus passed through the tunnel exit, a huge valley came into view with rows upon rows of grape vines. There were estimates that approximately 20,000 acres of land in the valley would support vineyard growth and that currently 10,000 were planted. Land values are reaching $25,000 per acre for a planted plot of land. Water is also an issue in that there isn't a river running through the valley, all watering and irrigation comes from wells and reservoirs. Another concern is that of frost. With the ocean so close, temperatures in October (their spring) can get dangerously close to freezing, creating many problems for flowering and budding plants. Despite all of these issues, apparently the soil conditions, sunlight conditions, and temperatures during the growing season are so ideal as to produce perfect wine grapes. More recently, Morande has been having success with their pinot noir growing in the region along with a few other secrets I knew of.

The bus cruised past the House of Morande restaurant, a new, modern-looking building set among the vineyards. That is where lunch was planned, but for now, we were heading for another vineyard owned by Pablo. Leaving the comfort of paved roads, the bus rumbled painfully down a gravel road through an electronic gate. A winding drive through rows of grapes vines led to a beautiful house with a pool, horses, and two waiting carriages. We got off the bus and were told that this was the summer home of Pablo. Several of us needed to find a washroom and we were told to enter the house. Opening the doors wasn't a problem as the house was wide open most of the year. After a welcomed break, our group headed into the back where the carriages were waiting. A taller, older gentleman resembling Pablo joined us. He was dressed in a pair of blue jeans and a plain blue shirt. This was Pablo's brother, Jorge, one of his eight brothers and sisters, and the only one working with him in the wine business. Pablo soon appeared and showed us his mud oven, the gentleman of Chile's Weber grill. A fire is built under the oven and you cook your empanadas, beef, etc. in this mammoth structure which had to be four feet in diameter. Proud of his home, but not at all a show-off, Pablo was in his element, and loving it. He seemed to enjoy having everyone surround him, making him the celebrity. Jorge, on the other hand, seemed quite comfortable in his role as the man behind all the action, keeping the vines producing their top quality product.

Two carriages were waiting to take us into the vineyards to look at the various grapes on the vines. We loaded up and headed out. Pablo's horse followed along side his carriage and Pablo once again had the look of an accomplished man in his element. Three stops were made in the vineyards so we could look and touch the varieties being grown. Sauvignon blanc, chardonnay, gewürztraminer and pinot noir were the ones shown to us. I believe that there were some sangiovese, nebbiolo or pinot grigio vines hiding somewhere in the vineyard as several of the Morande people have hinted about the company trying the Italian varieties on their lands. Our carriage drivers were dressed in the traditional Chilean cowboy outfit including the poncho. The huaso, the Chilean cowboys, looked quite convincing in their mantas, which weren't as colorful as the gauchos of Argentina, but seemed to fit quite well with the traditional nature of the Chilean people.

After our third stop, we headed back at a leisurely pace to Pablo's house. The bus was loaded and we were off to lunch. The temperature was cooling slightly as we neared the Pacific, but by now the sun had burned through the morning fog which rolls in every evening onto the valley floors. This natural air conditioning, coupled with the bright sun, is what makes the Casablanca valley such an ideal wine growing region. Peacefulness and serenity reign supreme out here.

The House of Morande restaurant was only several kilometers away as Jose, our driver, once again motored away. The warm sun shining through the windows of the bus made it difficult to stay awake. I was slipping into a light sleep when I saw the restaurant appear ahead...the nap would have to wait.

The House of Morande restaurant is situated in the middle of vineyard owned by Vina Morande. Their strategic presence is part of a campaign by the men of Morande to capture upon the upscale image...rich people traveling to Vina del Mar and the House of Morande. A perfect match! Anyway, the restaurant was obviously designed by a cutting edge architect. Its curving lines, stainless steel and wood, lots of glass and steel had a look and feel which said high tech. Our group stopped for the usual pictures and we soon saw Pablo Morande walking the grounds. Joining him was Juan Pablo, as usual, high energy and dressed for a business meeting after our lunch. I was getting to like Juan Pablo the more I got to know him. If he ever comes to the states, he would be welcome at my house. It looked like we were once again in for another high end treat. A menu was already prepared without any options for us to choose. Seating slowly took place and soon we were dining on sea bass carpaccio, a raw, thinly sliced sea bass covered with lemon, onions and herbs. Once again my first reaction was negative, but the food was terrific. Morande sauvignon blanc flowed freely from the anxious and attentive staff. The top brass was dining with us and service was exceptional. I was sitting at one end of the table near Jaime, Don and Jim. Dave and Mike were sitting across from me and we soon were laughing at the insane amounts of food and wine our bodies were absorbing. Soon, an olive oil was brought to the table, an oil which Morande will soon be exporting. The oil had a strong citrus flavor, yet it tasted good to dip our freshly baked rolls into the stuff. I reminded Jaime to insure that a case of the oil made its way to Chicago for Dave and me to share. A cream of mussel soup was next on the table and I believe a chardonnay was poured. It really didn't matter any more as large quantities of wine were becoming quite the norm for our three hour lunches. The soup was very good and I worked mine down to the bottom, leaving the mussels as a dessert for the dog or cat who was working the trash that evening. Dave, noting the two lone mussels, quibbled about trying new items and the line was drawn in the sand. I had to eat these suckers even if it killed me...and it almost did. Something about the texture of certain shellfish makes my skin crawl and mussels are on my short list of items to avoid. As much as I wanted to he-man those critters down, it just couldn't happen. I think Dave may have choked on his wine laughing at me, but it all didn't matter much anyway. Everyone was punch-drunk-tired and beginning once again to get intoxicated. Our next course, a cut of beef in some sauce with vegetables, made its way out. Pinot noir was poured and the feast continued. The warm sun was shining through the large glass windows. Pablo, Jorge, Jaime, Ximena, Miguel Luis, Juan Pablo, Macarena, and our cast of eight basked in the South American sunlight, enjoying incredible food, great wine and great company. Then a helicopter, a film crew and a local Chilean supermodel all arrived simultaneously. It appeared our afternoon luncheon was coinciding with several other newsworthy events. The House of Morande restaurant was *the* place to be. The helicopter landed in the back lawn and out jumped a Chilean woman (later identified as being from the Concha y Toro family) and the editor-in-chief of "Wine and Spirits," Joshua Green. He was in Casablanca to do a story on Pablo, Macarena and Morande. All eyes jumped to the lawn as the 'copter touched down on the perfectly manicured lush lawn. Out jumped Mr. Green and several others. Cameras flashed to catch the action and Pablo strolled out to greet his new guest.

Meanwhile, a film crew from Santiago was on hand to capture all the action for the 10 o'clock news. A film crew was trying its best to capture the stuff when another car pulled up with a local Santiago supermodel. She was being primped and polished by a group of gay men for some photo shoot on the grounds. The commotion level went from relaxed to high energy in a matter of minutes. Our group tried to be cool, but cameras began flashing as we tried to get the best shot of the action of the moment. The supermodel was reclining on the giant rocks, Pablo and Macarena were being seated with the crew from "Wine and Spirits," the local film crew was working to catch all the action as was our group. Jorge Morande seemed oblivious to the whole mess and sat with us for a few minutes before excusing himself for some other obligation. Pablo was the man of the hour in spite of his blue jeans and work shirt. Macarena was the proud daughter of the king, confidently working the press in her casual attire. These were working people who understood the wine industry, doing their thing. We watched in amazement at all the action around us.

Our group tried to finish our dessert when Miguel Luis went over to the supermodel. He said something to her and she got up and had her picture taken with me. She wasn't very pleased with the experience. Jaime was laughing, letting us know he was behind the prank. He apparently knew her producer from an encounter in the Napa Valley and he chose that opportunity for a little payback. The table seemed to laugh at us and our immaturity, while Pablo and Macarena were being interviewed at the center table, while the film crew from Santiago tried to get a news bit, while we tried to eat, while Jorge Morande just looked on. It was all getting tiring. I purchased a shirt for my wife and asked the Morande's to sign it which they all did without any hesitation. No one could find a dry marker so a black ink pen had to suffice. Soon everyone from our group had purchased bottles and were getting the famous Morande's to sign them, while they were getting interviewed by the magazine, while the supermodel was getting photographed, while the local news channel tried to get some shots, while the helicopter took off…Morande once again delivered an afternoon that we will all talk about for the rest of our lives.

There had been much action and it was getting late. It was time to board our bus. With another great meal and lots of wine in us, we loaded our trusty steed and bade farewell to the House of Morande restaurant. I felt sorry for those guests in the restaurant as they must have witnessed Americans at their worst. But, we'd had fun!

So we headed off to Valparaiso and Vina del Mar. A short illegal entry onto the highway by Jose and we were once again motoring along our way toward the ocean. Everyone in the group was tired and we drifted in and out of sleep for the next 45 minutes as we worked our way west to the old seaport town of Valparaiso. As a group, three days of eating and drinking was beginning to take its toll; we were toast. Next stop, Valparaiso…after I'd sneak in a quick nap.

Chapter 10

Wednesday, March 12, 2003

Valparaiso and Vina del Mar

A sleeping bus full of passengers was awakened to the sounds of Jaime welcoming us to the old sea port of Valparaiso. As we struggled to wake up, we were soon driving down the main drag of the town, along a make-shift city market in the median of the highway. Lots, and I mean lots, of tents were set up to the bustling trade of locals walking their way through the booths. I had read lots about Valparaiso, and for once, I didn't agree with much I had read. The town looked very old and very run down. Jaime informed me that he had lived in the town and was actually born in Vina del Mar, just a mile north, up the beach. Jaime did a good job pointing out the highlights of this old city, including the relocation of the Parliament during the Pinochet years. Schools, military offices and houses seemed to hang along the steep rock cliffs of this ancient town. Nothing looked remotely new. Many burnt out building and dirty streets helped hide any remnants of the beautiful town that could have existed here. Making matters worse was a warning from Jaime that this was a port town and that due to the unsavory sailors who disembark for shore leave, this was a town that needed your attention. Our guided tour went along for a while with a quiet bus in back. Not much was being said…and I'm not sure if everyone was still sleeping, or just wanting to get to our new hotel. The magnificent Pacific Ocean and its welcoming breeze were a sight to behold…welcome to Valparaiso.

A trip to this town wouldn't be complete without a ride in one of the city's famous elevators. There were about 15 of these ancient contraptions still in working order in the city, thanks in part to their world-wide status as an endangered historic site. We disembarked again to do a little shopping and ride the elevator. Jaime paid some amount of money, probably around a dollar or two for the 10 of us, to ride this thing up the side of a cliff. Crooked tracks, obvious lack of maintenance and an absolute lack of safety features, which we as Americans have come to expect and demand, were the order of the day. Despite my fears, our elevator performed flawlessly up the

150 foot incline. At the top, we were greeted by local merchants trying to sell their wares. None of them appeared exceptionally pushy, and Jaime had indicated a need to barter, yet I felt funny trying to knock a dollar off a ten dollar sweater that would sell for $70 back home. We worked the booths and once again needed to get moving. Bruce was actively buying, Dave struggling a little, and I determined to get a few things, even if I didn't get the best price. I grabbed Jaime or Ximena several times to interpret my negotiations. I ended up buying two Chile t-shirts for $5.00. I wasn't too sure of their quality, but they would look great on my kids. A washing or two could bring these shirts to their demise, but I was a happy consumer. I believed my Chilean shop keeper wasn't as happy with the deal as I was, but he wrapped my gifts and smiled graciously none the less.

Our bus was once again loaded as we began to negotiate the curvy and *very* hilly streets of town. Burnt out buildings side by side with beautiful government buildings set the tone for this old sea port town. We observed all the townspeople lowering the Chilean flag at exactly 6:00 pm, a tradition from years gone by. I was glad we were leaving the town to the north as dusk began to fall. I could only image what the streets would look like once the sun went down. We continued north along the ocean-front to the adjacent town of Vina del Mar.

No welcome to signs were needed to let you know you were leaving Valparaiso and now entering Vina del Mar. It was like going from cold to hot! Vina del Mar was everything Valparaiso wasn't, not the least of which was money. High rise hotels and apartments struggled for a view of the magnificent Pacific along a beach which many claim is as famous as the Copacabaña beach in Brazil. Vina del Mar is known as the city of gardens, and vegetation was everywhere. We slowed enough for a tourist class photo op at the "Clock of Flowers," a huge clock-garden overlooking the ocean. Jaime picked up the phone and said he was calling his mother as we drove by three large buildings. Sure enough, as we went by one of these buildings, a woman on the 10 - 15th floor appeared on her balcony, waving her arms frantically to catch our attention. I managed to shoot a photo of Jaime's mother, Elba, waving to the green tourist bus.

More kilometers passed as we moved out of Vina del Mar into the next big resort town directly to the north, Renaca. It was hard to distinguish where one town ended and the other began, unlike the experience from Valparaiso to Vina del Mar. More classy hotels and a fine beach, it could have been anywhere, but we had just entered Renaca. Our bus worked its way up a steep back street and we headed for our hotel. Everyone was beat and ready for some sleep. It was almost 7:00 pm.

The Conference Town had the look and feel of a modern hotel. Jaime told me we were originally going to be staying in the Oceanic Hotel, directly on the beach, but Morande couldn't secure enough ocean front rooms, leaving the Conference Town as their second choice. Our group labored into the lobby as our bags were unloaded from the bus. The only check-in requirement was a form needing basic information: name, company name, position and passport number. Not too difficult, and within two or three minutes, I had a room key, room 107, which made steps and elevators unnecessary, but I had heard bad things about security on the lower level of a hotel...I closed my drapes and blinds and got a safe key.

Conference Town could hardly be called anything less than beautiful, yet to me it somehow lacked the charm of Hotel Rugendas, more Holiday Innish. All was neat, clean and orderly when I checked in, but the room didn't offer itself to me as did our downtown Santiago location. Maybe it was the location of Rugendas, but it had charm, and my room location made every trip to the lobby, gym or restaurant effortless. I should feel ashamed for not loving this room, but to me is seemed a step down from our first location. I later found out that my sentiments weren't shared by most. Most of the members of our group seemed to see the Conference Town as an equal, or upgrade. I unloaded my suitcase and tried to settle in. Dinner call was in half an hour and we had agreed to meet in our building's sitting room. On the bus ride over, I told Jaime to invite his mother to join us. He said she couldn't and despite my persistence, Jaime kept saying no.

A hotel clerk was trying to light a fire in the gigantic fireplace in the main seating area as I strolled in several minutes late. Don and Dave had each brought some wine down from their rooms for everyone to sample. This was a trend which I am happy to say seemed to be growing in popularity. Our group gathered around four couches in the sitting room and began sampling wines...too much tannin, not enough fruitiness, shallow, not well balanced...yes, this was wine snob country at its best. We didn't take the conversation too seriously and had lots of fun with our new friends. A woman bearing a striking resemblance to Jaime appeared with a tall American man; this was Jaime's mother, Elba Jones, now on her tenth marriage (at least according to Jaime). They sat with us and enjoyed conversation and wine while we wasted away an hour getting ourselves ready for dinner. Despite our fatigue and hunger, I don't think anyone would have given up the conversation. Our group was tight and we were friends, and friends just like to talk and drink wine, and that's what we did!

Finally, it was time for dinner. I didn't remember the exact time when we strolled across the courtyard to the dining room. Our first order of duty was to find the local Internet access. Several of us on the trip had grown quite used to its presence, and I wanted and needed to hear from Carmen. Dave, Tom and I found an old IBM computer in a small room off the conference center, the Internet connection was working, albeit it a little slow, but at least we could communicate. (We heard calling from others in our group as we needed a group photo.) The restaurant was empty, only us and a group of pilots were in the cavernous room. The pilots (English, I believe) made several remarks about tourists and my shorts ("Ee really got dressed fa dinner, Aey?") It angered me, but I shut up. Jose, our bus driver was asked to join us. No one cared and I think everyone was actually glad to have him. He negotiated our bus down dirt roads and through the busiest and narrowest streets of Santiago. He was one of the gang.

Our choices for dinner this evening was a French Onion soup or a salad, Conger eel or stuffed turkey and one of several desserts. As you may remember, I had given up on desserts. Just bring them out and chances were very good I would eat them...*all*. Wines for the evening were chardonnay, pinot noir and sauvignon blanc, cabernet sauvignon and merlot. Lots of bread and another ad hoc discussion about Morande, friendship and life. I chose a salad for starters. The lighter greens, sliced avocado, cucumber (I think) and onions tasted refreshing. At Jaime and Mike's suggestion, Conger eel would be the entrée of choice. It was excellent. Served with steamed vegetables. Dessert, well, more sweet stuff. We were a tight group. Jaime offered Jose a toast for being such a good driver. We laughed and talked wine industry, Pablo, and life in the states and Chile. Nothing seemed off limits, nor were any remarks taken too seriously. A few jokes, another toast, more wine, dessert, more wine, more jokes, a few pictures. I was thankful that there was only one more formal dinner in Chile after this evening as I didn't think I could take much more. At 12:00 several began to break off, heading for their rooms. The time looked right and I made my exit as well. It was almost 2:00 in Chile, midnight back home. I was tired, but still felt the need to continue this journal while everything was fresh. I had managed to shoot over 200 images which would someday be incorporated into these words to paint a picture of the wonders of Chile I had been blessed to experience. I hope that one of my Chilean friends comes to Chicago someday as I feel I owe them a place to stay, dinner and to meet my family.

Jaime had promised us a low key day tomorrow. A beautiful drive up the coast to a resort town, maybe some swimming in the ocean, and we wouldn't have to leave till 10:00 am. Sleep in a little, enjoy a slow morning, whatever.

I headed back to my room and my heart began its usual evening aching for my family. I did miss them, but our journey was coming to an end.

Chapter 11

Thursday, March 13, 2003

Traveling north to Zapallar

I woke up this morning at 8:00. Sleep hadn't been the problem it can be for me back home. Despite all the wine drinking we were doing, I had yet to wake up feeling like I've had too much to drink the night before. Exercise crossed my mind, thank goodness, only briefly. I was tired, so a shower and off to...eat some more. Today we had been promised a tourist day and I knew it would be received well by all of our group. We needed a break from this wining and dining.

My Chilean Wine Odyssey
A Week Touring the Wine Country of Chile

An overcast sky and cooler temperatures was my morning reminder of the neighboring Pacific. Often a morning fog rolls in and the bright sun can take several hours to burn through. Off to breakfast, where once again I found Dave typing away at his PC. The buffet line at the Conference was similar, but it was not quite as extensive as at the Rugendas. Service was also a little slower. Coffee was what I needed and the waiter was more interested in talking with the seniorita than getting me my joe. Jaime, Tom, Bruce and Dave soon joined us and told of their continued antics of the previous night at the pool table. I was glad I had chosen bed, and Jaime looked as he probably could have quit a littler sooner himself. Our bus was leaving on a loose knit drive up the coast in an hour so a little down time would feel good. Straighten up to my room, type a little, organize a few pictures…you know, traveling kind of stuff.

The bus was loaded and off we went. First stop the local beach. The sky still filled with fog and overcast, I had on jeans and a jacket and was glad I did. Walking up the soft sand with the magnificent Pacific Ocean slapping at your feet was a wonderful and humbling experience. The surf was calm this morning but knowing the next major land mass to the west was thousands of miles away was beyond the imagination. The cool breeze felt refreshing. The bus was loaded and we began our journey north along the coastal highway. The word "highway" is used loosely as this was a two lane affair only in fair condition. Along our way we took a photo op and tasted a local snack roll called a baroquely (par que yo). It reminded me of a fortune cookie rolled into a thin tube.

Our trip continued along the road north with traffic quickly becoming non-existent. The vast difference in class became quite obvious. Small shelters that barely qualified as houses against vast estates, fenced, to ensure the privacy the wealthy owners expected. Most views of the ocean were fenced off to maintain the privacy of the owner. Giant fronts of glass rose up mountain sides to enjoy unimaginable view of the mighty Pacific. Sunsets would be a sight to behold from these magnificent palaces.

Second stop, a private country club to enjoy a stretch of the legs and our first glass of wine for the day, some sauvignon blanc. I had grown to enjoy sauvignon blanc more than any wine on our trip. Its versatile, light, drinkable nature made it my favorite. The country club was a members-only affair with a gated entrance. The club house was a huge hacienda, with 12 x 12 beams of cypress and eucalyptus. Small details such as inlaid rock, wonderful woodworking and breathtaking views and patios made this a special place indeed. Chilled sauvignon blanc was soon swirling in our glasses as we talked and looked in amazement of what the well-heeled in Chile could enjoy. The health club looked over the golf course with a view of the Pacific in the background. Money is an amazing thing.

The bus loaded and we continued our trek north to the town of Zapallar. The pace today was much slower. A late start and lazy walking were the norm. It was already 1:30 and the bus was still working its way along the winding and hilly roads to the exclusive resort town of Zapallar. The narrow roads were lined with beautiful homes, all overlooking the ocean. We were dropped off by a long walk along an ocean front path to our restaurant. Ornate dwellings, many showing their German heritage, lined the ocean front. Glorious patches of flowers hung along the steep cliff walls while the ocean splashed playfully along the beach. No guardrails here, you step off the edge and you fall to an unpleasant stop against the rocks beneath. I am sure my wife would have been nervous here!

Our restaurant appeared on a point several hundred yards down the path. Chiringuito was a place out of a movie. Giant slabs of cypress served as tables. Pieces as wide as 36 inches by 4 inches thick…chairs cut from logs, all perched along the ocean's edge. The walk around the back side of the restaurant had the heads of our soon to be lunch gasping for their last breaths, obviously in vain. Lunch today was off the menu, the first time a prepared menu wasn't on hand. A discussion was had on some topic, while pisco sours were once again ordered by all. An icy cerveza helped hydrate me and several others. Soon it was determined we would order several appetizers, several salads, and each pick our own main entrée. Razor clams served piping hot with parmesan cheese were first. I had my first encounter with raw shell fish only several weeks ago, but the razorbacks were very good. Nothing fishy to make things nasty, just great flavor. A Chilean salad was next and for a main course, the Reineta was the fish of choice. Jaime described this creature of the sea as a close relative of a halibut. Grilling was the choice method and sauvignon blanc and chardonnay began to flow. Mike was awarded a special "El Capo" boat. He was thrilled and I caught the perfect photo that captured his excitement. I knew I'd been drinking a lot of wine as this morning I found myself swirling and sniffing my water glass! Lots of thanks and toasts continued as we sat for several hours enjoying the surf and food. The few restaurant guests seemed quite annoyed by the loud Americans, but one by one they left until we were the only ones left. A family with a small daughter from England happened in as our lunch was winding down, but they didn't seem to mind our antics. More pictures and more talk and we began the walk down the remainder of the path to catch up with the bus, which had moved to the end of the winding trail. We enjoyed the mile long rugged walk along the beach.

Tidal pools seemed to interest several of us and we climbed our way down the rocks and searched. Certainly no Brookfield Zoo display, but Bruce and I managed to find some wildlife. Bruce dragged up a small crab. This poor crab unfortunately found its way down the back of the shirt of Miguel. Both Miguel and the crab survived the experience. A dolphin worked its way up and down the coast searching for food and the wonderment of the ocean hit home, as did the reality that our dream trip was coming to an end. A slow stroll along the path had some inspirational moments as the infinite nature of our world seemed to diminish our significance; for thousands and millions of years these waters had crashed upon the rocks we were climbing. We are but mere grains of sand in the hourglass of life. The beaches were deserted as we enjoyed the slow walk back to the bus.

I headed to the computer and checked e-mail one last time. Letters from my boys made me glad I was going home soon. A lot still had to be done and I was looking forward to our meeting in Valparaiso tomorrow morning.

Chapter 12

Thursday, March 13, 2003

Dinner in Vina del Mar

Tired, yes indeed. I was closing in on exhaustion. There is only so much wining, dining and sightseeing one can do and still drink so much wine. One by one we met in the lobby and awaited departure for our final dinner. At 8:00, we loaded our bus, Jaime was on time, (for once) and took the 15 minute bus ride from our hotel in Renaca to the Portofina restaurant in Vina del Mar. The energy level began to build as the bus drove down from our hill-top perch and the beautiful night sky along with the Pacific came into view, through Renaca into Vina del Mar. The restaurant was once again an attractive place, loaded with wines from Chile in all sizes in display cases by the front door. Walls were decorated with Chilean celebrities, similar to the restaurants in Chicago which show off their celebrity guests. The host identified several to me, the only one of which I had heard of was Emilio Estafan, husband of Gloria Estafan. We were directed to a private dining room with a splendid view of the ocean. As we filtered into the room, Jaime suggested having our pisco sours outside on the veranda. Another pisco sour, I was getting pretty good at these things. We poured onto the terrace and broke into our groups. Jaime's mother spends half of her life in Vina del Mar, the other in Atlanta, as she is married to an American, Bob Jones. We pushed Jaime (it really didn't take too much pushing) into asking mom and Bob to come along. They, too, were part of the group. It was easy to see where Jaime got his sharp wit and good looks.

Conversations once again began to start; we knew our time in Chile was nearing its end. Bruce and Dave, Tom and Don, Jaime and his mother and Bob, Mike, Jim and Dave, Ximena and I. We switched partners like a high school dance. Enjoying our newfound friendships, the final countdown towards home was here. Appetizers were brought out. A skewered beef and chicken served with mayonnaise and a mustard sauce was sampled while we enjoyed our sours under the South American evening. The temperature was probably in the 70's as a gentle breeze blew in from the ocean. I think everyone was trying to somehow put the last few days into perspective, still enjoying the evening, but knowing our good-byes were inevitable. By 9:00 pm we were called into the dining room where appetizers were awaiting. Octopus, another first time for me), calamari, more razor clams and bubbling hot scallops with garlic were waiting to be enjoyed with some chardonnay. I gobbled down some bread, only to have Dave Masson politely remind me that I had just eaten his food. Everyone laughed and told stories of the week, as the group began to talk more about what had happened as opposed to what was going to happen. We all signed a sheet giving our address and e-mail information so that we could exchange contacts, leads, stories, photos and whatever else when we got home. More toasts and lots and lots of laughter. Despite not wanting to drink too much with such a busy day tomorrow, more pisco and wine were on their way.

We were going to order from the menu and Jaime did his normal comedy act as he read through the menu in a mocking voice, translating and recommending all at the same time. Our seafood choices included sea bass, conger eel, Dover sole, albacore and several others. I chose conger eel, grilled, with hearts of palm and tomatoes. As I had come to expect, it was outstanding. Mike (now affectionately known as "Capo") had turned us on to this ugly fish/eel, but the stuff was really good. Grilling brings out the best in it. More laughter and desserts filled the table. Not one, two or three, but five or six different taste treats. Sticking with my travel books, I stayed away from the fresh berries, but most of the others didn't care. Dave asked Jaime about the chances of getting sick and Jaime responded "Not a problem, besides, you are leaving tomorrow, so I don't care." Typical Merino.

Soon, straight pisco appeared on the table. I declined, but even Jaime's mother began to pressure me. One by one toasts and memories were exchanged and the friendship was rolling along at great heights. Jaime gave his emotional thank you. Miguel Louis gave his, Ximena hers, Dave, Mike, Don…the list kept going. It was once again a great night with great new friends. Chile would always be in our hearts. Jaime also let us in on a secret; while at the House of Morande restaurant the other day, Joshua Green, the editor in chief of Wine and Spirits told him secretly that the 2002 House of Morande sauvignon blanc would be named a value buy in the upcoming issue. This was the same wine we drank at our wine dinner in Chicago! A crown jewel of an award which should bring much attention to Morande USA and make Jaime's job difficult as the 2002 vintage has already sold out!

John R. Knuth

By midnight it was truly time to leave. There was talk of going to the casino, but I knew it was beyond my means, mostly physically at this point. The bus loaded and a vote was taken and it was an easy win for the hotel. We had an early appointment with the Minister of Economics and needed to check out of the hotel by 8:30 am. Some had already packed, but I hadn't, and I knew I needed some time to get my thoughts down for the evening. A group photo with everyone displaying the Pablo Morande peace sign, Don speaking in espanol, Jaime singing…just more fun from some slightly over served, slightly overage guys having a great time. No strippers or foul language were needed to keep us straight. This had been a class act from the beginning and it would end that way as well. We dropped off Jaime's mom and headed back to the hotel where there was talk of a repeat pool game, but I quickly got out of range and headed for my room.

As I sat typing I was torn between knowing I was leaving tomorrow and missing my family so much, at the same time knowing I would have to say good-bye to my new friends. It had been a wonderful week, but it is time to go home. I would miss this.

Chapter 13

Friday, March 14, 203

Goodbye to the Pacific

An alarm clock didn't come as standard equipment in our hotel rooms and I knew it was late when I went to bed last night. Waking every half hour or so to check the time became the norm, so I ended up deciding to get out of bed at 5:45 am. I still had to pack and lots needed to be done. As I lay in bed, I was astonished by the deafening silence. There was absolutely no noise. A shower, then I packed my stuff. Our time in Renaca was quickly coming to an end. Our meeting this morning had been moved up to 9:00, so the morning rush would soon begin.

John R. Knuth

A knock on the door, I figured it was Dave checking in for breakfast…I was right on half of my assumptions. It was Dave, but looking rather pale, he indicated he had spent most the previous evening in and out of bed, and in and out of the bathroom. He was hurting. I had packed some Immodium AD for just such a problem and he soon was powering down a tablet or two to get things under control. Knowing we had three hours of bus travel and more than 12 hours of air travel and countless hours waiting made the timing of the illness much worse. One by one as our group appeared in the lobby, they immediately sensed Dave's condition and put their own conditions on the back burner. It seemed as if several of our group had come back to the hotel the night before and instead of calling it a night, stayed up late and talked, and drank, and drank some more. Jaime, Don, Jim, Bruce and Mike all looked a little more tired than usual. I was glad that I had chosen the bed route, as my own stomach was beginning to do some aerobics. Our itinerary was for an early morning stop at the office of Minister of Economics for the fifth region. Due to Chile's long length, the country is divided into regions, similar to states. The fifth region was a prime position as Valparaiso was the country's second largest city and contained the country's largest sea port. In addition, the affluent seaside towns of Vina del Mar and Renaca, to name a few, were within its boundaries. The bus ride with all its stopping and going was anything but comfortable, especially for Dave who had taken the front perch on the bus. The minister's office was a short ride from our hotel and we were soon in the midst of the bustling port town of Valparaiso for our meeting.

The building was a taller affair, looking as if it was built in the early 50's. All I saw was a single elevator serving the building. The minister's office was on the 19th floor and it would be sure to command an impressive view of the city. A cramped ride in the diminutive elevator with 11 of us stuffed inside made me appreciate elevator inspectors back in the states. Nothing suggested anything less than adequate performance, but I wondered none the less. The doors opened to facilities which looked more appropriate for a small town mayor, but certainly adequate and efficient. We were introduced to the minister, Pablo Zuniga. He was much younger than I had imagined and at first thought he might be the assistant to the real minister. I was wrong. We later learned that the President of Chile had "cleaned house" and replaced the old ministers with younger, highly educated individuals. The gentleman we had met was only 32 years old. A handsome man, impeccably dressed. We began the discussion with a tour on the balcony. It was an impressive sight as the warm sun basked on our view of the Pacific, the port and the various hills that make up the unique town. Next we were led into a conference room where two impressive booklets were handed to us, the first on Chile, the second on agribusiness in Chile. I would like to report that the presentation was good and well worth the effort, but knowing the length of travel ahead of us and having had plenty to drink the night before, I looked at my fellow travelers and didn't feel as badly about my occasional "head bobs" and eyes closing under their own weight. The presentation was informative, but the minister's absolute lack of English forced all discussions to be handled through our tour guide and interpreter, Jaime. The discussion seemed to last forever, but in reality about 45 minutes. Mike, at the risk of being threatened with visual daggers from everyone, asked a few questions but began to the feel the heat from his peers and saved his remaining questions. We thanked the minister for his time, hit the banyos and headed outside for a picture. Dave, looking a little better, again took the front perch and we were back on the road.

Our next destination was back to the Casablanca Valley for lunch at the House of Morande restaurant. It wasn't my first choice, not because the food or the ambience wasn't excellent. I had begun to mentally check out. The sun was warm and I drifted off for a quick nap on one of the few smooth roads in Chile. The sound and feel of Jose slowing to exit woke me and we were soon on the grounds of the House of Morande restaurant once again. Jaime told us that Pablo would be joining us for a light lunch. He was on his way and would be here in a half an hour. I was hungry and my stomach rolling. Chilled sauvignon blanc was brought out and the thought of a drink didn't sit too well. I had waived off the first round and opted for a Coke and a melon juice, but accolades of the wine made me motion the waiter for the second round. It did taste good and the refreshing wine under the glorious sun felt good. The wait went by quickly and Pablo once again made his entrance. He was pleasant and recognized our faces. One by one we posed with him on the edge of the vineyards while flags of Chile, Morande, Casablanca and the US waived proudly in the background.

Lunch was a simple affair with quartered sandwiches prepared on flatbread. It was nice to not have the huge, lengthy affairs we had been having, and we were back on the road by 2:00. Naps were the rule for the one and one half hour ride back into Santiago.

A word about driving in Santiago. Fast and close. I wouldn't have wanted to drive a micro car between these guys, yet they seemed to do it without much fuss at all, while pedestrians ran across the streets and occasional stray dogs wandered as well.

John R. Knuth

The program for the remainder of the afternoon was going to be a stop at the local artisan center, then back to the hotel, where Jaime had a room for us to change into our airlines clothes. The artisan center was like a huge park, filled with hundreds of booths with local artisans hammering out copper, carving wood, knitting sweaters, you name it, they were making it. The pace in the place was very low key. I was looking forward to visiting here and my only wish after getting here was that we would have allotted more time. A lot of junk, but also lots of very beautifully crafted pieces of jewelry, hand carved woods and stone, paintings, just dozen upon dozens of little stores with no pressure to buy. You could look and touch, but no one seemed to mind when you would just give thanks and move on. I managed to find a few last minute gifts but was still looking for a lapis bracelet. Earlier in the week I had been to a high end jewelry store and found something I liked, but didn't purchase it at the recommendation of Jaime until I had checked out the goods here. Miguel Louis, Tom, Dave, Bruce, Ximena, and Mike were with my group. Everyone checked out items and used Miguel or Ximena to do the negotiating. I learned quickly that Miguel was much more interested in doing the price debating. I had seen some things for my son, James, and was ready to buy. The amount of my purchase came to roughly $10.50 US. I was ready to give the woman in the booth $15 just to get along with things when Miguel started going to bat for me. It wasn't that I didn't appreciate his fierce loyalty, is just didn't matter to me. Miguel insisted we leave, and we did. Time ran along and I still couldn't find a necklace. Our bus was scheduled to leave the grounds and head back to our hotel at 5:30 pm. We would clean-up and depart for the airport at 6:30. An hour drive to the airport would get us there at 7:30, approximately two hours before we were scheduled to depart. I wasn't satisfied with the look or feel of any of the jewelry at the market and I wanted to buy a more substantial piece. I needed to go back to the jewelry store where I had been earlier in the week. Jaime, Mike and Ximena and I had all been given cards at the store with specific instructions to call the store at any time and they would send a cab, pick us up and take us back. Time was running out. We couldn't find Mike or Jaime and my card was in my bags. Ximena sat down and began making cell phone calls.

A side note...cell phones seemed to work so much better in Chile than in the US. I can't tell you the number of times a phone would ring in the absolute middle of nowhere, with mountains all around. Near or far from people or places, the Chilean cellular phone system is vastly superior to ours.

Miguel Luis began pumping me up in his broken English to insist on a better price. The store was known for not being too willing to negotiate, but Miguel wanted a piece of them. The problem was he couldn't speak enough English to conduct the final deal. Time was running out and Ximena reappeared from around the corner. "A cab is on its way," she announced. I was getting nervous as traffic was heavy. It would be quite possible to get caught in a fierce rush hour and mess up the remainder of the plans for our group…and the cab was late. Miguel was insisting that we fight to lower our price. He kept banging his clenched fist into his open hand. I got it. Mike was going to go along and we were going to do a bulk deal, but he opted for any icy cerveza under the shade of an umbrella. Ximena offered to broker the deal and we left. The taxi driver was proud of his English and explained that he was under contract with the jeweler. He went on to explain the five different grades of the stone and that what I would be looking at would be a superior product. I was nervous as time was running out. The cabbie, like any good local, knew of side streets to by-pass much of the heavy traffic and within minutes we were at the store. I had explained to Ximena that I was more interested in a long-term quality piece than just getting something. She understood. On the way over to the store she commented that Dave and I were quite different. Dave was much more willing to show his feelings and I would hold them in more. She thought it was very thoughtful (who was I to disagree) to stick to my guns and go for the piece I felt better about.

Anyway...once back inside I was offered a pisco sour, but no time for that today. I quickly went back to the room where I had seen the piece that had caught my eye. With the words of Miguel Luis still in my mind, I made my offer. "Not possible" was the clerk's response as interpreted through Ximena. I raised both hands to suggest that was my deal. She said "CASH." I was amazed at the quality of her English. I shook my head yes, she headed in the back room, then re-appeared and said something to Ximena in Spanish. Ximena nodded and the deal was done. I didn't regret my decision. The jewelry store was packed. I was guessing Brits, Aussies and Americans from the various voices I heard. I received a thumbs up from a older woman from Texas. She said "the little lady back home oughta like that!"

The cab was still waiting outside and a quick cab ride to the hotel had beaten the bus back. Don had chosen to not go to the market and was in the lobby. Time was nearing for our journey to be over. We both shook our heads in amazement over the week's events while Ximena waited outside for the bus. Jose motored in just minutes behind with everyone unloading for one last time. Jaime's room would be available for a quick clothes change, bathroom needs or whatever. I grabbed my bag and headed up to the 9th floor to change into jeans for my flight. Jaime's room was much nicer than mine, which was also very nice…so this was how the other half lived. Minutes later, Dave appeared trying not to act panicked, but looking for his bag with his notebook computer and passport inside. He said, "I'm not freaking out yet, but I am starting to get close." For the next 15 or so minutes, everyone joined in for the hunt. The conclusion became more and more obvious with every passing minute. Dave clearly remembered loading several booklets into his bag just before getting off the bus, all under the watchful eye of a woman who saw him moments before Dave got off. She probably saw the large group gathering around the back of the bus while our driver unloaded the items and made a dash. Within seconds, Dave's PC, camera, pictures, passport, palm pilot and memories, were out somewhere on the streets of Santiago. A crime of opportunity. The mood in the camp quickly changed. Jose felt bad.

Despite the financial loss, which could easily top $3000, Dave's passport and pictures were also gone. The pictures would most likely never be retrieved, but the passport became the more immediate issue. We were to be leaving the country within the next three hours. Would the color photocopy Dave had in his wallet, along with his itinerary and Illinois driver's license, suffice? Under these trying times, no one, especially Jaime was sure. Miguel wasn't going to the airport with us, so with our sad faces, we gave our farewells to him. He handed me a pin that he called his offering of friendship. I thanked him and hugged him. I really like Miguel Luis, he is a class guy in any country.

The bus loaded up in a much different mood. There was total silence on the bus as everyone was saddened by the event and Dave worried if he would be going home. Jaime made a call to the US Embassy where the news wasn't good. The feeling at the Embassy was that he wouldn't be able to go, but to try to work with Delta, maybe they could work something out.

Making matters worse was that the Embassy was closed on Saturday and Sunday. The next day Dave would be able to get in to talk with someone would have been on Monday. Then, if he was able to square things up, he would catch the late evening flight out Monday night. Three more days in Santiago when you were ready to go home, plus another painful trip to the airport on the bus. This wasn't looking good.

I could go on and on about the dramatics which played out over the next hour or so, but due to a little luck, good back up documentation and Jaime's knowing the Delta supervisor, Dave was allowed to board. A brief meeting with the International Police (I didn't even know they existed.) and it was confirmed. A big sigh of relief, but now the pain of the missing photos and equipment hit home.

As we worked our way through security for the last time, we gave our farewells to our new friends from Chile. Miguel had given his farewells at the hotel and now Jaime and Ximena did the same in the lobby of the airport. One by one, hugs and thanks were exchanged. We all wished things could have been more upbeat as it appeared an inappropriate way to end such a wonderful week, but we all knew in our hearts how we felt. Our friends in Chile had outdone themselves. I offered my home to all three if they were ever to be near Chicago. I would make a trip and find the time to repay them for some of the hospitality and class they showed us.

We disappeared through security and it was finally time to go home. At the check-in gate, Dave and I put in one last sympathy attempt with the gate attendant, hoping to get a free upgrade to first class. The space was worth the price (big talk). It didn't appear to be working, so Mike, Bruce, Dave, Tom and Jim headed off for a quick bite to eat. French fries would have to work as time was running out. Just as we began to eat, a local repair man began re-gluing a broken stair runner with some mineral spirits. The smell was awful, making our departure much easier. Our plane was now loading.

Chapter 14

Friday, March 14, 2003

The ride home

Another sold out flight. It would be cramped and unfortunately we knew what we were in for. In reality, it was horrible, but not unimaginably so. The flight attendants on Delta were very efficient, but not very friendly. On this trip, Dave was stuck in the middle of the middle section, well towards the back of the plane. I at least had the ease of entry and exit of the aisle seat, but no matter how you slice it, coach class just isn't made for people over 5' 10" tall. Harry Potter made the ride home a little more bearable, but it was hard. I know I drifted in and out of sleep many times, but no matter how hard I tried, I couldn't get comfortable. I had known from our flight down that working on the PC was all but out of the question. We did our best, checking in with our fellow travelers on the occasional trips to the back of the plane to stretch our legs.

Due to favorable winds, our flight home was only 9 hours long. I was once again reminded of the wonders of our world. Only a century ago the same trip would have taken months, and if you would have survived, you certainly would have lost some weight, not gained some with airline food and drinks. I can only imagine what the next 100 years will bring.

In Atlanta, we once again did the security thing. The security in Atlanta was the best I have seen yet. Friendly, very thorough, you didn't mind, and actually were glad that these guys were doing their thing. After rechecking our luggage for the return flight to Chicago, we began giving our good byes to our fellow travelers. Ten hours in a plane and the sympathy towards Dave's loss made these good byes a little shorter, but not any less sincere. For eight guys that had just met, we had done a great job of getting along and making the most of our trip. Obviously, the wonderful treatment made it much easier, as did single rooms!

John R. Knuth

For Dave and I it was a short trip through the gigantic Atlanta terminal and a brief wait to board our plane to Chicago. Much to our surprise, the plane was scheduled to leave 10 minutes early in an effort to stay ahead of traffic which was backing up at O'Hare. We boarded early, but once again, an overbooked flight kept us at the gate for at least 30 minutes more than we wanted.

Once in the air, conditions were again cramped. We were tired and just wanted to get home. The actual flight went well, but ground delays in Chicago kept us turning and holding high above the city at the whims of the Chicago air traffic controllers. We touched down in Chicago at about 9:30 am. Baggage appeared on time and we remembered where I had parked. No one had damaged my truck and it started without hesitation. A $91.00 parking fee reminded me I was back home, but I didn't mind. Dave commented on how roomy an S-10 pickup felt. I couldn't have agreed more. The sun was beginning to burn through the fog and we were on our final leg home.

Chapter 15

Some days later

Putting in all into perspective

A week has passed and I am sitting in my home. There is no place like home! Despite my having a wonderful trip, my heart never stopped thinking of my family back home and how I wished they could have been with me to experience the wonders of Chile.

I chose to not write this chapter on the trip because I wanted an opportunity to reflect upon what I had experienced after the "glow" had worn off. I am not sure the glow is gone, as I hope a small piece of it will always live on, but a few days back at work and it seems like the entire adventure was an eternity ago.

Chile is a country of extremes...extreme wealth and poverty, extreme mountains and valleys, extreme warm and cold, extreme wet and dry...the list could go on and on. I was fortunate enough to be traveling with a group of extremely accomplished individuals. Their commitment to their work, family and friends was powerful. I believe the fine people of Morande will go places and reach their goal of being the driving force behind the Chilean wine industry.

The Chilean people were a quiet people, very much to themselves. My first impression was that they weren't very friendly. A simple "hello" on the street would often invoke an "Are you talking to me?" look. I learned that this wasn't arrogance, but shyness. I believe it. Dress and behavior are very conservative. This wasn't Brazil.

Chilean food was simply great. I was fortunate to experience foods such as conger eel, marluza, corvina carpaccio, razor clams to name a few. I experienced the pisco sour, and wouldn't mind having one here by my side as I type these final words.

But I believe my most lasting memory of Chile will be of our hosts, the good people at Morande. Starting with Jaime, whom I couldn't help but like the first time I met him at Lincolnshire Country Club, where he was the host for our Foundation Dinner and Wine Tasting. His charisma and charm are undeniable. He is a contagious individual.

My new friends in Chile, our travel companions, Miguel Luis and Ximena. Despite Miguel's limited English, we communicated quite well. His passion for his friends and attention to details was evident in everything he did. I believe I have a good friend in Miguel. Ximena was also a wonderful person. Many women may have been intimidated by being the sole female on a trip with ten other men, but Ximena never wavered. As such, I believe she was treated with respect by all the members of our group. Her help with interpreting and explaining sights along the way was great and appreciated very much.

Juan Pablo...his enthusiasm was never ending. I believe if he were to be living in the States, he would be a friend of mine. His smile was infectious.

John R. Knuth

Luis Matte, next time you are in Chicago you can take my motorcycle for a ride anywhere your heart desires. Anyone with five kids deserves that!

Pablo, Jorge, Macarena and all the others at Morande, your enthusiasm, professionalism and love of what you are doing is evident in everything you do.

Passionate. That is the word I believe sums up my Chilean wine odyssey. Every person I met associated with Morande was passionate about what they did. I believe the reason we were invited to Chile was to capture just a fraction of the passion these people have for their work and life itself.

As for my travel partners, well guys, I'll miss you. For a handful of strangers who met in a small waiting room in Atlanta, Georgia, we had one heck of an adventure.

An open invitation stands to my new friends. I welcome an opportunity to show each and every one of you a fraction of the hospitality and friendship you gave me during my few days on my **Chilean Wine Odyssey.**

Chapter 16

Future Recommended Readings

Also by Author: John R. Knuth

My Italian Wine Odyssey

A Journey Through the Wine Country of Northern Italy

Hope to see you there!

Printed in the United States
1499700005B/206